"This book explains the fundamental components of human memory, such that both students and educators can understand and apply the material directly to learning. The text explains not only how memory works, but how we can utilize that information to optimize learning across a broad swath of domains. I look forward to using this book in my own courses in educational psychology."

—Anne Cook, Ph.D.,
Professor and Chair of Educational Psychology
Department, University of Utah, USA

"Memory in Education makes a substantial contribution to the educational literature by articulating how theory and research explain and support multiple memory techniques. Among the many useful aspects of this text is the discussion of cognitive load theory. Knowing how to reduce extraneous cognitive load and increase positive, 'germane' cognitive load is especially important in addressing the complex information demands in education today. There is much in this text that can benefit both students and teachers."

—Marc M. Sebrechts, Ph.D.,
Wylma and James Curtin Professor of Psychology,
The Catholic University of America, USA

Memory in Education

As our understanding of the human memory system broadens and develops, new opportunities arise for improving students' long-term knowledge retention in the classroom. Written by two experts on the subject, this book explores how scientific models of memory and cognition can inform instructional practices. Six chapters guide readers through the information processing model of memory, working and long-term memory, and Cognitive Load Theory (CLT) before addressing instructional strategies. This accessible, up-to-date volume is designed for any educational psychology or general education course that includes memory in the curriculum and will be indispensable for student researchers and both pre- and in-service teachers alike.

Robert Z. Zheng is Professor of Educational Psychology at the University of Utah, USA.

Michael K. Gardner is Professor of Educational Psychology at the University of Utah, USA.

Ed Psych Insights

Series Editor: Patricia A. Alexander

ROBERT Z. ZHENG
MICHAEL K. GARDNER

Memory in Education

Routledge
Taylor & Francis Group

NEW YORK AND LONDON

First published 2020
by Routledge
52 Vanderbilt Avenue, New York, NY 10017

and by Routledge
2 Park Square, Milton Park, Abingdon, Oxon, OX14 4RN

Routledge is an imprint of the Taylor & Francis Group, an informa business

Library of Congress Cataloging-in-Publication Data
A catalog record for this title has been requested

ISBN: 978-0-367-02856-5 (hbk)
ISBN: 978-0-367-02857-2 (pbk)
ISBN: 978-0-429-01914-2 (ebk)

Typeset in Joanna
by Apex CoVantage, LLC

Contents

The study of memory is one of the most important areas of psychology. Without memory, we would be lost in the present with no sense of who we are. Memory is also an essential component of learning. Our memory of past educational experiences creates the schemas and knowledge structures we use to make sense of current lessons. Education is a cumulative process, building on the past and making future understanding possible. Memory is the cornerstone of education.

Somewhat surprisingly, students and teachers often have only a partial sense of how memory operates. In this book, we present the theory behind the psychology of memory and how that theory relates to better learning and instruction. In Chapter One, we present the argument for the importance of memory in education with some examples of how memory can go awry. In Chapter Two we present an information processing model of memory and the processing of information. Information enters the mind through the sense organs and then spends a brief period of time in sensory memory. There is likely one sensory memory for each of the senses. Information that is attended to is moved to short-term memory or working memory. The earlier short-term memory model emphasized the storage of information, whereas the later working memory model emphasized both storage and manipulation of information. For information to be stored for more than a few minutes, it must be transferred to long-term memory. Working memory and long-term memory differ in ways other than how long information is retained; working memory is dominated by phonological and visual codes, whereas long-term memory is dominated by semantic codes. In Chapter Two we also cover a number of distinctions made by psychologists: (a) declarative versus procedural knowledge; (b) controlled versus automatic processes; (c) explicit versus implicit memory; and (d) semantic versus episodic memory. We also describe the developmental course of working memory and long-term memory as this will be important to teachers in designing effective instruction.

In Chapter Three we focus on the implications for learning that derive from the information processing model. In particular, we describe numerous methods for successfully transferring material from working memory to long-term memory, including rehearsal, rereading, distributed practice, categorization, mnemonics based on visual imagery (i.e., the keyword mnemonic, the method of loci, and the peg word method), imaging material in texts, verbally mediated mnemonics, and summarization of textual material. We also discuss highlighting and underlining, a method commonly used by students whose efficacy research does not support. We also discuss the issues surrounding how to retrieve material stored in long-term memory. The issue here generally involves having a sufficient number of effective retrieval cues. Techniques such as elaborative interrogation, self-explanation, and practice testing help students develop connections among new information and already learned information so that the new information can be retrieved via multiple retrieval routes. We present the idea of large-scale knowledge structures—schemas, scripts, and frames—and their importance in learning. Finally, we described metamemory, which is our knowledge of our own memory processes and how to use these effectively. Metamemory develops throughout childhood, making older children more effective learners than younger children.

In Chapter Four, we introduce cognitive load theory. Given that our working memory resources are limited, learning tasks can consume those resources in different ways. Some of those ways are beneficial, but some are not. Intrinsic cognitive load derives from the complexity of the learning task at hand. It is determined by the number of interacting elements in the material to be learned. Extraneous cognitive load refers processing demands of a learning task that are not necessary but result from poor instructional design. Redundant and repetitive information can consume processing capacity while serving no instructionally useful function. Finally, germane cognitive load refers to processing that is used to build new information and cognitive schemas. Although in most instances we seek to reduce intrinsic cognitive load and eliminate extraneous cognitive load, we often wish to increase germane cognitive load as this is the load that produces learning.

In Chapter Five we describe strategies for dealing with cognitive load in instruction. Six strategies are outlined for reducing intrinsic cognitive load in teaching: (a) pretraining, (b) concept maps, (c) worked examples, (d) schema-induced analogy, (e) cognitive prompts, and (f) knowledge automaticity. All of these strategies help provide the required background knowledge that learners need to more easily deal with the complexity inherent in learning materials. Six additional strategies are presented to reduce extraneous cognitive load in teaching: (a) visual-visual strategy, (b) visual-auditory strategy, (c) keyword-auditory strategy, (d) visual proximity strategy, (e) visual-auditory strategy, and (f) cueing and signaling. Although not all of these strategies will apply to each instructional situation, these lists will provide teachers with a set of research-validated procedures for dealing with the harmful effects of cognitive load. For germane load, instructors will generally want to increase this type of processing. Five additional strategies are presented to enhance germane cognitive load: (a) learner control, (b) self-regulated learning, (c) multiple perspectives, (d) collaborative learning, and (e) technology using artificial intelligence (AI). Most of these strategies can be adapted to different subject matters and grade levels. Finally, Chapter Six ties together the themes of the book and puts its content into perspective.

The material presented in *Memory in Education* should help students become more effective learners and teachers become more effective instructors. The material is based in theory, research validated, and useful for learners across the developmental spectrum. We hope you will enjoy reading it as much and we have enjoyed writing it.

Acknowledgments

We would like to thank all of those who gave generous support and assistance in the journey of this book project. Our thanks go particularly to our series editor Dr. Patricia A. Alexander, who oversaw the conceptual framework and the content structure of the project since its inception. The book would not come to its present form without her wonderful support and guidance.

Our appreciation also goes to our editor, Daniel Schwartz, and editorial assistant, Katie Paton, at Routledge for their professional support and patience. We would also like to thank the publishing team at Routledge, who have demonstrated the highest level of professionalism and integrity.

Last but not the least, we would like to thank our families for their understanding and support and for their tolerance of the hours at work necessary to complete this meaningful project. Robert would like to thank his wife, Sharon, and children, Joanna and Henry, for their love and unwavering support. Their encouragement, trust, and occasional friendly jokes have made the process of writing a pleasant journey. Michael would like to thank his wife, Beverly, and his children, Kaitlyn and Kelly, for their love and support. It is perhaps no surprise that they have all majored in psychology at some point during their academic careers.

Robert Z. Zheng and Michael K. Gardner
University of Utah, USA
February 2019

One

Introduction

The process of education involves the acquisition of skills and knowledge on the part of students who are facilitated by a teacher. At the heart of education is memory. Without memory, we wouldn't recall what we had learned during the past day or month. Our previous knowledge could not inform our current and future learning. We would be left adrift in the present.

Usually learners attempt to connect new material with older material already stored in memory. But memory can be a fickle thing. Sometimes it is triggered in faulty ways. One of us was returning from a trip to Princeton, New Jersey. After a two-hour drive, he stopped at a burger chain to get some lunch. He ordered a cheeseburger and a cup of coffee. He picked up a packet of salt for his cheeseburger and a packet of sugar for his coffee. But, in his tired state, his skills were triggered incorrectly: He put the salt in his coffee and the sugar on his cheeseburger! In this situation many things were correct: There were two packets of white granules that needed to be added to two food items, and memory contained a skill for adding granules to food. However, the packets and their desired target items were interchanged in his automated skill, and the result was an inedible meal.

In a second example of memory gone awry, one of us was at a professional conference in Boston. While walking to the convention center, an attractive young woman approached him, and said, "I know you." This caught him by surprise. He had no memory of the woman at all. At first, he thought the woman was mistaken. But then she used his name. Who was this woman who seemingly knew him well? Eventually, she said her name, and indeed he did know her. She was a former master's student who had gone on to become an attorney. She had married a psychologist who was attending the conference. Why had his memory failed? In this case, the cues to her identity (other than her appearance) were missing. The context for meeting her was completely wrong. In his mind, he had encoded her as an attorney in his home city. The usual cues of the professional psychology conference and Boston turned up nothing when he searched his memory. Perhaps this has happened to you as well: You have failed to recognize someone because the context in which you met him or her did not match the context in which you expected to see the person.

Memory is an essential part of education. The knowledge and skills stored in our memories must be brought to bear to make sense out of the lessons we are studying. A skillful teacher can activate these memories so that they are available for use in the classroom. She or he might ask students to remember a previous trip to a forest prior to a lesson on photosynthesis. Likewise, a good student can create new memories and tie these memories to previous knowledge through the use of good study techniques. For instance, a student studying the causes of the Second World War might ask him- or herself whether each cause is similar or different from previously learned causes of the First World War. If a student wishes to recall material in the future, then this material needs to be tied to past learning though numerous meaningful paths or memory cues. Questioning similarities and differences to prior learning is one method of building these paths.[1] This is the reason that rote rehearsal (simply saying something to yourself over and over again) is a poor memory strategy (although many students engage in it). Although the new material may be strengthened in memory, it is learned in isolation and not tied to what the student already knows.

To learn effectively, it helps to understand how memory works. Psychologists have learned a lot about memory over the past 150 years. In this book, we will try to provide you with an overview of the psychology of memory. We will discuss a generic information processing model of human memory. This will describe how information enters the mind and how we process that information. We will then present more information about two of the memory systems in the model: working memory and long-term memory. We will also discuss the idea of cognitive load and how load impacts memory. Throughout we will also try to tie this knowledge to how to be a more effective learner or teacher. The more you understand about memory, the better you can use your memory to be an effective learner.

Two

Information Processing Model of Human Memory

During the 1960s, cognitive psychologists began to explore how people process information. They were heavily influenced by the advent of computers and tried to identify similarities between human information processing and computer information processing. The process went something like this: (a) environmental stimuli exist in the external world and are detected by sensory organs such as the eyes, ears, nose, and skin surface; (b) this sensory information is held briefly in a sensory memory so that it can be identified as meaningful objects, and so on; (c) the identified information is stored in a time-limited, short-term memory—here the information can be transformed and processed; (d) the information can then be transferred to a relatively permanent long-term memory, where it can be stored until needed in the future; and (e) the information in long-term memory, combined with information in short-term memory, can give rise to responses, which is the way the individual effects his or her environment.

By 1968, this had been summarized by Richard Atkinson and Richard Shiffrin into what has been termed "the modal model of memory" (see Figure 2.1).[2,3] As can be seen in the figure, human memory had been divided into three qualitatively different types of memory. It is perhaps best to discuss each of these memory stores in greater detail.

How does forgetting occur in sensory memory? One way, outlined earlier, is through the simple passage of time. As time passes, the information in sensory memory fades away. Another way is that information in visual sensory memory can be overwritten by new information. In an experiment by Averbach and Coriell, a grid of letters was presented briefly (50 milliseconds), and a single letter was later cued by either a bar marker above the letter or by a circle surrounding the letter.[5] In the bar marker condition, results were similar to those found by Sperling's partial report method.[4] But for the circle marker, results were worse than simply asking participants to recall all the letters. It seems that the visual system had treated the circle cue as a solid disk, and it overwrote the letter it was intended to cue. Thus, new information in sensory memory can overwrite and displace older information.

SHORT-TERM MEMORY/WORKING MEMORY

Atkinson and Shiffrin's Short-Term Memory Model

For information in sensory memory to be interpreted (i.e., to have meaning associated with it), it must be transferred from sensory memory to working memory. In Atkinson and Shiffrin's model this was referred to as "short-term memory."[2,3] Short-term memory is a temporary storage area where a limited amount of information, say seven plus or minus two units, can be held for a limited amount of time, say 20 seconds.[6] The size limitation refers to coherent units of information. So, short-term memory can hold approximately seven random letters (such as r, b, x, etc.). But if the letters are organized to form words (such as cat, tree, house, etc.), short-term memory can hold about seven words (which will clearly be more than seven letters). In effect, short-term memory can hold seven plus or minus two organized units of information.

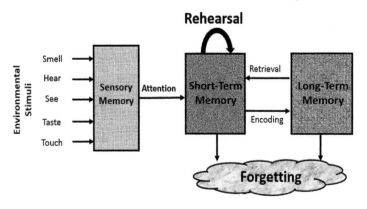

Figure 2.1 The Modal Model of Memory

SENSORY MEMORY

When external information enters the information processing system, it is held by a sensory memory. There is likely a sensory memory for each of the senses, but the two most extensively studied sensory stores are those for visual and auditory information. These are sometimes referred to as iconic memory (for the visual system) and echoic memory (for the auditory system). The existence of a sensory memory was demonstrated in a number of experiments performed by George Sperling.[4] Prior to this time, psychologists had demonstrated that if an individual were briefly presented (say for 50 milliseconds) with a relatively large number of items (say 12 letters) and asked to report them, he or she could recall only four to five items. This was referred to as the "span of apprehension": the number of different things a person could simultaneously attend to. But participants in these studies reported something strange: They could "see" more of the letters than they could report. By the time they had written down the first four to five items, the others had faded away.

The experiment cited here was an example of "whole report": The participant was told to report everything he or she had been exposed to. Sperling realized there was a way to test the size of a participant's iconic memory without resort to whole report. His technique was called "partial report," and it follows the same principle as a test. He presented participants with three rows of four letters each. However, instead of asking participants to report everything they had seen, he presented them with a cue tone that could either be high, medium, or low in pitch. If participants heard the high tone, they were to report only the top row. If they heard the medium tone, they were to report the middle row, and if they heard the low tone, they were to report the bottom row of presented letters. The idea was that no single row of letters exceeded the number that participants could report under the whole report technique, so any fading of sensory memory should not impair their recall. However, the subjects could not know which row was to be tested on any given trial of the experiment: they could direct their attention only to that aspect of their visual sensory memory after the display had gone blank and the tone had sounded. Sperling found that people got approximately three out of four letters per row correct. Thus they had access to something more like nine letters in visual sensory memory, which was nearly twice the size estimate under whole report conditions.

Sperling also varied how long after the display went off it took for the cue tone to sound. The idea here is that until the tone comes on, the best strategy would be to try to remember all the letters. Once the tone occurs, the participant can focus their attention on the correct row and report just those letters.

At some point in time, when everything in visual ▮ memory has faded away, getting the tone will be no ▮ than being told to report all the letters. How long does ▮ for visual sensory memory to fade away? Sperling's co ▮ sion was 250 milliseconds, or a quarter of a second.

This leads us to the properties of sensory memory. ▮ it is truthful. It records the sensory stimuli from the ▮ ronment as they actually occur, subject to the limitat ▮ of our sense organs. Second, it is relatively large. Appro ▮ mately 9 out of 12 simultaneously presented letters. Third ▮ is relatively brief—one-quarter of a second for visual sens ▮ memory. Estimates for auditory sensory memory are lo ▮ ger: from 250 milliseconds to 15 minutes depending upo ▮ the experimental paradigm used. To the extent there is any consensus, 2 seconds seems reasonable. The longer estimates for auditory sensory memory may stem from the fact that auditory information is spread out in time, whereas visual information is spread out in space. This requires the auditory system to hold onto sensory information longer so that it may be integrated into a larger-scale unit. Finally, at least for visual sensory memory, it is without attached meaning. The sensory memory store contains raw sensations. For meaning to be attached (e.g., to know the letter name of "A"), the sen- sory information must be transferred to short-term memory and integrated with previously learned information in long- term memory. People can attend to physical dimensions of the visual display (attend to the top row when they hear the high tone), but they cannot, for instance, attend to just the vowels. Doing so would require them to identify the stimu ▮ by transferring each to short-term memory, and the resu ▮ would be no better than telling them to report all of the le ▮ ters in the display.

These units are sometimes referred to as "chunks." This leads to a useful strategy to expand one's short-term memory capacity: chunking smaller bits of information into larger meaningful units. If you were trying to remember a list of numbers, say 1, 7, 7, 6, 1, 8, 1, 2, 1, 8, 6, 1, 1, 9, 1, 4, 1, 9, 4, 1, this would be an extremely difficult task. However, if you chunked the numbers into 1776, 1812, 1861, 1914, and 1941, the task would be much simpler. Combined with a little knowledge of U.S. history, you could remember the long list of digits as the dates of the beginning of five wars the United States had fought in.

The brief duration of short-term memory was demonstrated in experiments by John Brown and Lloyd and Margaret Peterson.[7,8] In one of these experiments, individuals were shown three consonant trigrams (e.g., RZM, XBT, CWN) followed by a random three-digit number (e.g., 492). Participants were to count backward by threes from this random number until they were cued to recall the three consonant trigrams. The purpose of the counting task was to prevent participants from saying the trigrams to themselves during the memory period. The results show that after approximately 18 seconds, recall was at approximately 15%. Most of the information had simply faded away (numbers and letters were considered sufficiently different so that interference of the numbers with the letters was considered unlikely).

There was one way to keep material active in short-term memory that was stressed by Atkinson and Shiffrin: rehearsal.[2,3] If you could say the material to yourself again and again, it would not fade from short-term memory. So if you're ordering a pizza, and you look up the phone number of the pizzeria, you would likely repeat it to yourself until you'd dialed the number. According to these authors, the longer material was kept alive in short-term memory, the greater the likelihood that it would be transferred to long-term memory. Although under many circumstances this is true, it is not a particularly efficient learning technique. Repeating material to yourself over and over again is referred to as rote learning. Meaning is not involved. As we will discuss later on, making to-be-learned information meaningful and relating it to what you already know are much more efficient learning techniques.

The other control mechanism in short-term memory that Atkinson and Shiffrin described in detail was transferring one information code into another. When verbal material is typically presented to individuals, it is presented visually (of course speech is presented in auditory form). To rehearse verbal information, the visual code must be converted to an auditory code. This was demonstrated in an experiment by Conrad (described in Glass and Holyoak, p. 7).[9,10] Conrad presented college students with lists of six letters each, which they read silently. When they were asked to recall the letters from short-term memory, the errors they made were acoustically similar to the presented items (C was recalled instead of B) rather than visually similar to the presented letter (X was recalled instead of V). Participants had converted the visual information into auditory information. Interestingly, Conrad found that deaf participants made errors that were visually similar rather than acoustically similar.[11] It appears that deaf individuals do not typically convert visually presented verbal information into an acoustic code.

Levels of Processing

Atkinson and Shiffrin also mentioned that short-term memory had a few other control processes, for example, decision-making and using retrieval strategies to bring information from long-term into short-term memory, but relatively little was said about them. Some psychologists proposed that the emphasis in memory should be on what we do with information rather than what storage system it was in.[12] They proposed the *depth of processing* model. According to these researchers, what determined memory was how deeply information was processed. If information was processed in a shallow fashion—for instance, attention was directed on the typeface in which words were presented—little would be remembered after a short time. However, if information was processed deeply—for instance, attention was placed on the semantics (or meaning) of presented words—a great deal would be remembered. Experimental results supported their conjecture: Focusing on meaning produced better recall. However, the level at which information was processed was never defined in a precise, independent way. The model simply stressed that what we do with to-be-learned material will play a critical role in our memory for it.

Baddeley and Hitch's Working Memory Model

In 1974, Alan Baddeley and Graham Hitch provided a new model of short-term memory, which they called "working memory" (see Figure 2.2).[13,14,15] The original working memory model consisted of a central executive linked to two independent slave subsystems: the phonological loop and the visuo-spatial sketchpad. In the working memory model, there was a much greater emphasis on the processing of information. The central executive allocates attention to the slave subsystems and coordinates the operation of working memory. The individual slave subsystems are tailored specifically to verbal material and visual material, respectively.

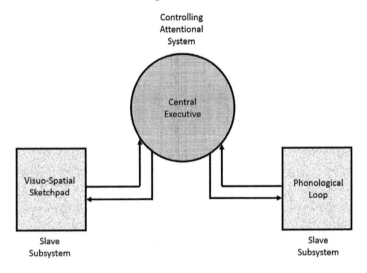

Figure 2.2 Model of Working Memory

There are some interesting research results that support the validity of the individual slave subsystems. With regard to the phonological loop, there are four empirical sources of support. The *phonological similarity effect* shows that short-term memory of phonologically similar items (e.g., PGTVCD) will be harder than phonologically dissimilar items (e.g., RHXKWY). This occurs because the phonological loop is based on phonological coding of information, and phonologically similar items have similar codes that are easier to confuse. The *unattended speech effect* shows that when participants are asked to immediately recall visually presented digits, speech and speech-like sounds (which participants are to ignore) interfere with digit recall. This is because the digits are converted to their names and stored in the phonological loop. Speech sounds enter the loop and interfere with the participant's ability to rehearse the digits. The *word length effect* states that the number of words that can be held in short-term memory is related to the length of the words (i.e., the number of syllables they contain). Memory span appears to represent the number of words you can utter in about 2 seconds. *Articulatory suppression effect* refers to the fact that when participants in a memory study are asked to repeat an irrelevant item, such as repeatedly saying the work "the," they are able to remember less than when they do not repeat any item. Articulatory suppression occurs because the phonetic information in the irrelevant item enters the phonological loop, takes up space there, and interferes with the participant's ability to rehearse the relevant information.

There is also research to support the existence of the visuo-spatial sketchpad. Lee Brooks developed a task that could be presented either as a visual or a verbal task.[16] The task was the same in both cases; only the method of solving it changed. Baddeley, Grant, Wight, and Thomson had participants solve both versions of the Brooks task, either alone or while performing a pursuit rotor task (tracking a spot of light moving erratically in a general circular pattern).[17] The results showed that the pursuit rotor task did not interfere with the verbal version of the Brooks task but interfered significantly with the visual version of the Brooks task. In this case both the visual Brooks task and the pursuit rotor task were competing for the limited resources available in the visuo-spatial sketchpad.

In a more recent presentation of the working memory model, Baddeley has added a new component: the episodic buffer.[18] The episodic buffer allows the central executive a way to combine visual, spatial, and verbal information to form complete percepts of the type we might encounter in our everyday experience. Clearly something like a trip to the coffee shop involves more than separate visual and verbal information. It involves the amalgamation of sight, sound, smell, and taste. The episodic buffer is where this type of information is stored and manipulated.

In conclusion, short-term or working memory is where information is held and manipulated for relatively brief periods of time, say 20 seconds to a few minutes. Here it can be connected with already known information and transformed in various ways. The goal is to prepare at least some of this information for a more permanent type of storage.

LONG-TERM MEMORY

Long-term memory differs in significant ways from short-term or working memory. It is extremely large, large enough to contain all of the memories we've accumulated over a lifetime. Some psychologists think it is infinite in capacity. Others think there must be some limits as there are only a finite number of neurons in our brains and only so many ways that they can be interconnected. From a practical point of view, any limitations of long-term memory are not due to its size. It is big enough to do its job for our entire lives.

Long-term memory is also of essentially unlimited duration. You can probably recall moments from your childhood, even if you are well into adulthood. The question of whether everything you ever learned is still in your long-term memory is a difficult one. Two possibilities exist: (a) Everything is still in long-term memory, but you may not be able to access the information at the current time; or (b) some of the information has faded away with the passage of time and is no longer in long-term memory. When Loftus and Loftus asked 169 individuals which possibility they thought was true, 84% chose the first possibility and 14% chose the second possibility (2% gave some other answer).[19] So why do people, especially psychologists, favor the first position? One reason is due to a series of studies performed by Wilder Penfield and his associates.[20,21,22] Penfield was a neurosurgeon, and during surgery to remove regions of the brain that were producing epilepsy, he would stimulate the cortex of patients (who were awake at the time). These patients often reported vivid memories from their past (e.g., "That was Uncle Louis playing the piano at a Christmas party when I was eight.") that they were hitherto unable to recall. This research led people (including Penfield) to conclude that almost everything we are exposed to is stored in long-term memory, although we may not be able to access it at a given point in time. Loftus and Loftus cast doubt on this interpretation, however.[19] They note that of 520 cases in which Penfield stimulated the temporal lobe of the brain, only 40 (7.7%) had a memorial response. Why didn't the stimulations all produce memories? We don't know why. But more problematic is that we don't know if the vivid memories that patients recalled were true memories or confabulations of some sort: Perhaps sounds and sights that the mind combines into something that feels very much like a valid memory to the patient. So, although Penfield's findings have influenced many generations of psychologists' beliefs about the permanence of long-term memory, the support is far more equivocal than many realize.

Another piece of evidence sometimes used to support the fact that everything we experience is stored in long-term memory is spontaneous recovery of previously learned material.[23] Sometimes we remember something that we were previously unable to remember—it's been spontaneously recovered! This definitely proves that there is more in our long-term memories than we can recall at any given point in time. But is it all in there? Spontaneous recovery is difficult to study in the lab because of its nature (it occurs spontaneously). Psychologists have studied related issues such as *tip-of-the tongue phenomenon* (the failure to recover something even though some characteristics of the missing item can be recalled) and *prompted recall* (giving people a cue after they fail to recall some items).[24,25] Tulving and Pearlstone found that in a categorized free-recall task (remembering a list that contained 10 fruits, 10 kitchen items, and 10 automobile brands), providing participants with the category names after their initial recall attempt helped them remember additional items that they couldn't recall without the cues.[26] These phenomena demonstrate that there is more in long-term memory than we can recall at any point in time. However, the question of whether everything we experience is in long-term memory is an open one. It is difficult to prove a negative: that something is not in long-term memory! Despite this, the size of long-term memory is not a practical constraint when it comes to remembering large amounts of information. For practical purposes, the size of long-term memory is unlimited.

Although sensory memory is dominated by sensory codes and working memory is dominated by acoustic and visual codes (i.e., the phonological loop and the visuo-spatial sketchpad), long-term memory is dominated by semantic coding. Information in long-term memory is organized by its meaningful relationships to other information in long-term memory. One model of long-term memory is that it is a large collection of nodes that represent concepts that are connected to other nodes via labeled relational links.[27,28,29] Thus the node "chess" is linked to "game" by the labeled link "play," and "robin" is linked to "bird" (by the link "subset") and to "orange" (by the link "color of"). Two nodes, or concepts, are semantically similar to the extent that they share a large number of links, either direct links or links through intermediary nodes. Thus, individual species of birds (e.g., sparrows, robins, and wrens) are highly semantically similar as they share many links (e.g., wings, feathers, beaks, and the superset category of bird). Likewise, colors are highly semantically similar. But bird and color are less semantically similar as there are fewer aggregate links between these two nodes (although there are some: oriole to orange, cardinal to red, etc.).

In this model of long-term memory, the basic process is the activation of nodes by retrieving them from long-term memory into working memory through the process of attention. Consider the question, "Is a bat a bird?" Bat, once attended to and activated, will spread activation to related nodes such as "fly," "nocturnal," and "lives on blood." Bird will also spread activation to a set of nodes, such as "fly," "has feathers," and "has wings." The individual will attempt to answer the question by judging the number of nodes activated in common, along with a consideration of whether any particular nodes are required by the definition of bird: in this case, "has feathers." Because birds must "have feathers," the respondent would answer no to this question.

Activation spreads from the original node in working memory to other nodes, and from those nodes to still other connected nodes, but it does not spread indefinitely. With each link farther from the node of origin, the level of activation is decreased. Finally, at some number of nodes/links from the original node of activation, the amount of activation available falls below the level necessary to bring the new node into consciousness. These distantly activated nodes may be raised to a higher level of activation than their base level, but the individual is not aware of them. However, this increased activation may make them easier to activate by other nodes spreading activation, and thus they may be more likely to "pop into mind" via other thoughts.

Given what we've said so far about spreading activation, consider the following two tasks: (a) Name a fruit that begins with the letter P; and (b) name something that begins with the letter P that is also a fruit. Which task is harder? The answer is the second one: Name something that begins with the letter P that is also a fruit. Why? Once a node is brought into working memory and activated, activation spreads through all of the nodes connected to it. Think of this like pipes connected to a central water source. The more pipes that are connected, the less water will flow down any one of them. Likewise, the more links that are connected to any node, the less activation can flow down any one link to the next node. When asked "name something that begins with the letter P" activation begins spreading from the node for P. Many, many things begin with the letter P, so activation must be divided by a large number of links. However, when asked "name a fruit," activation begins by spreading from the node for fruit. Although there are a great many fruits, there are far more things that begin with the letter P. Thus the activation flowing down the links from fruit is stronger, making that question easier to answer.

To summarize, long-term memory has three important properties: (a) It is of essentially unlimited duration; (b) it is extremely large; and (c) information is organized semantically (by meaning). This does not mean that we can easily access everything in long-term memory. Like an attic, if everything stored there is clearly labeled and organized, finding what you need is a breeze. But if the material in long-term memory is poorly organized and its meaning is unclear, finding the thing you're looking for can be difficult or impossible. Examples of organization can be found in studies of recalling lists of words. Bousfield presented participants with a list of 60 words composed of 15 words from each of four categories (animals, names, professions, and vegetables).[30] The 60 words were presented randomly, one word at a time, for 3 seconds per word. When participants recalled as many words as they could from the list, the words tended to cluster into words from individual categories (even though the words were presented without regard to category membership). The meaning of the words affects how we retrieve them. A word from one category tends to bring to mind another word from the same category. The category names themselves can also serve as cues for remembering additional words. Thus, long-term memory is organized around meanings rather than the sounds of words or how they look visually. When items lack meaning and organization (say remembering telephone numbers for distant relatives), it is difficult to store the information in long-term memory for quick recall.

SOME COMMON DISTINCTIONS IN THE MEMORY AREA

Declarative Versus Procedural Knowledge

Normally, when we speak of memory in education, we are thinking about memory for factual information, such when the Battle of Hastings took place (1066 A.D.) or who was king of England during the American Revolution (George III). Psychologists refer to this as "declarative knowledge": factual information that can be called into conscious awareness.[31] There is, however, another knowledge we possess which psychologists refer to as "procedural knowledge." Procedural knowledge is demonstrated by an individual's performance on a task. Examples of procedural knowledge are your ability to ride a bicycle or drive a car. This type of knowledge is difficult, if not impossible, to call into awareness and put into words. Indeed, trying to do so often interferes with the performance of the skill, as when a golfer begins to "think too much" about his or her swing, making the swing even worse!

Procedural knowledge begins as declarative knowledge but is transformed into a procedure for performing the skill with practice. Fitts and Posner described three stages learners pass through in acquiring motor skills.[32] First, the learner is in the *cognitive stage*. During this stage the learner refers to the instructions for the task, and it is these instructions that guide performance. Next, the learner enters the *associative stage*. During this stage connections among the elements required for successful performance are strengthened, and errors in the understanding of the task are gradually eliminated. The outcome of the associative stage is a procedure for performing the skill. At this stage the procedural skill and the declarative knowledge about the skill may coexist in memory. Finally, the learner enters the *autonomous stage*. With additional practice at the skill, performance becomes automated, speed increases, and accuracy is enhanced. At this stage, performance is governed by the procedural knowledge, and the declarative knowledge about the task fades away (i.e., you forgot the rules but perform the task correctly). Although Fitts and Posner were describing motor skills, the situation is quite similar for cognitive skills.[31] For teachers, enhancing learning involves the development of both declarative and procedural knowledge. Factual knowledge is important in becoming more expert in any field. However, skills, such as how to use laboratory equipment in the science lab, are equally important in developing expertise.

Controlled Versus Automatic Processes

Along the same lines as the declarative/procedural knowledge distinction, psychologists distinguish between controlled and automatic processes. *Controlled processes* consume our attention and/or working memory capacity. We can perform only a few controlled processes simultaneously; after that we have exceeded the capacity we have available. At that point we are forced to either switch back and forth between the tasks (increasing the time necessary to complete the tasks) or incur errors in our performance of the tasks. An example of a controlled process would be counting backward from a random three-digit number.

However, if the conditions are right, we can convert a controlled process into an automatic one. An *automatic process* consumes little to no attention or working memory capacity. We can perform an automatic process with other controlled processes without performance decrements. Examples of automatic processes are comprehending language and driving a car (for a skilled driver!).

In reality, there is a continuum of automaticity from completely controlled tasks to completely automated ones. Many processes can become automated with enough practice. A set of studies by Schneider and Shiffrin demonstrates this fact.[33,34] These researchers had participants look for a target letter or number among a series of visual displays. The displays (on different trials) could contain either one item, two items, or four items. When participants were looking for a number among letters (or a letter among numbers), they could achieve 95% accuracy within 80 milliseconds, and the size of the visual displays (one, two, or four) did not affect performance. Individuals in this condition were essentially automatic in their performance. But when participants were looking for a letter among letters (or a number among numbers), they required 400 milliseconds to achieve 95% accuracy, and their performance declined as the size of the display increased from one item to four items. Individuals in this condition were performing the task as a controlled process. Why? Our extensive experience with language has made distinguishing numbers from letters automatic. But distinguishing one letter from another (or one digit from another) is not automatic.

In another experiment, these same researchers always chose a target letter from the same set of letters (B, C, D, F, G, H, J, K, L) and the nontargets from a different set of letters (Q, R, S, T, V, W, X, Y, Z). Individuals at first performed the task (of finding one letter in a set of other letters) as a controlled process. But after 2,100 experimental trials, they had learned to distinguish the target group from the distractor group, and they performed the task as an automated process. So, practice can transform a controlled process into an automated process (if the mappings of letters to target and distractor group remain constant throughout practice).

Automated processes are generally known as *skills*. Skills take time to develop through practice and become faster and more accurate during the process of skill development. Eventually the skill can become automatic, no longer consuming cognitive resources. But skills deteriorate with lack of use. However, it usually takes far less time to relearn a skill that has gone dormant. Kolers compared the performance of participants reading normal text to reading inverted (upside-down) text.[35] At first, participants were fast with normal text (1.5 minutes per page) and relatively slow reading inverted text (16 minutes per page). After 200 pages of practice, the speed of reading normal text remained the same, but the speed for reading inverted text had dropped to nearly the same speed as reading normal text (1.6 minutes per page). The participants returned to the lab after 1 year (during which they presumably hadn't read inverted text) and were retested. The speed of reading normal text hadn't changed, but the speed of reading inverted text had declined (to 3 minutes per page). Although their newly learned skill had eroded, it took them only 50 pages of reading inverted text to return to their prior rate (1.6 pages per minute). So, skills deteriorate without practice. But once learned, they can be reinstated with far less practice than it took to originally develop the skill.

Explicit Versus Implicit Memory

When students take a typical test, they are asked to identify the correct answer from among a set of alternatives (i.e., a multiple-choice test) or to produce an answer to a question from memory (e.g., an essay test). These are examples of *explicit memory*: "the test makes explicit reference to, and requires conscious recollection of, a specific learning episode" (p. 501).[36] This is the most common type of memory we deal with as teachers and students.

There is, however, another type of memory that can be demonstrated. *Implicit memory* is the expression of information that was previously encoded "without consciousness or deliberate recollection" (p. 501).[36] This type of memory seems much more mysterious, and it can operate in ways different from explicit memory. An example of implicit memory, described in Schacter,[36] involves the famous Russian psychologist Sergei Korsakoff. Korsakoff investigated a type of amnesic syndrome in which individuals could not recall events of the recent past (they were unable to transfer new information from short-term memory to long-term memory). However, Korsakoff described an amnesic woman patient to whom he had previously administered electrical shocks.[37] He returned on another visit carrying the case that contained the machine used to administer the electrical shocks. Although she had no memory of previously meeting him, she commented he had probably come to administer shock therapy. Thus, she had an implicit memory for the shock machine, even though she had no explicit memories of seeing it in the past.

Implicit memory can also be seen in the pioneering work of Hermann Ebbinghaus.[38] Ebbinghaus found that participants who learned a list and subsequently forgot it were faster to relearn the list than were participants learning a new list. He referred to this phenomenon as "savings." This would seem to be an example of implicit memory, but it could be possible that upon relearning, participants recognized the list that they could not recall (in which case, savings might be due to explicit memory). However, in more recent research, Nelson showed savings for items that participants could neither recall nor recognize, which suggests that at least some savings is due to implicit memory.[39]

Warrington and Weiskrantz (see also a description in Roediger[40]) conducted a series of studies with patients suffering from anterograde amnesia: which is to say that these patients could not remember new information once it had left short-term memory.[41,42] Psychologists felt that these individuals were simply incapable of transferring information from short-term memory into long-term memory. Warrington and Weiskrantz had these amnesiacs perform four tasks. Two of the tasks were explicit memory tasks: recalling items that had been presented on a list and recognizing items that had been presented on a list. The other two were presented as guessing games and were measures of implicit memory: naming fragmented words in which each letter was degraded and completing words when given three-letter stems (i.e., tab for table). The actual words to be named had been presented earlier in the experimental session, but obviously the amnesiacs had no memory of them.

The results of these tasks provided an interesting picture of the deficits of these patients. Compared to controls, the amnesiacs were impaired on the explicit memory tasks. This is not surprising because this is the definition of amnesia. But the patients were essentially the same as the controls on the implicit memory tasks. Thus explicit memory could be impaired while leaving implicit memory untouched!

The question still arises as to whether explicit and implicit memory can function differently in normal, non-impaired people. The answer seems to be yes. Experimental manipulations that affect explicit memory in one way can affect implicit memory in a different way. An example is a study conducted by Larry Jacoby (see also a description in Roediger, 1990[40]).[43] Participants were tested in one of two ways. Either they received an explicit recognition memory test in which they were to pick out words on a list that had been previously studied, or they received a perceptual identification test in which they were shown the same words as on the recognition memory test but very briefly (30 milliseconds each) and had to read the words aloud. The latter test was an implicit memory test: Participants did not have to remember the words, but if there was an implicit memory for them, the task of seeing and reading the briefly presented words would be easier. Jacoby manipulated the conditions under which the participants studied the words. They could be presented outside of a meaningful context (e.g., xxx-COLD) or in a meaningful context (e.g., HOT-COLD) or generated from a meaningful context (e.g., HOT-???). The context was always an antonym, and participants almost always generated the correct word from the context.

The results of this study were quite interesting. In the explicit memory condition (the recognition memory test), participants were best in the generation condition, next best in the meaningful context condition, and poorest in the no context condition. This finding was already known and is referred to as the "generation effect." Jacoby had simply replicated it. However, in the implicit memory condition (the perceptual identification test), the order of conditions was completely reversed! The no context condition was best, followed by the meaningful context condition, finally followed by the generation condition. Thus, it seems as if implicit memory may be governed by rules quite different from those of explicit memory.

Semantic Versus Episodic Memory

Another distinction commonly made is between semantic memory and episodic memory. Both of these types of memory reside in long-term memory. *Semantic memory* is our memory of everyday things and how these are organized.[31] So, we know that sparrows are birds, that plates are used to hold food, and that plates, forks, knives, and spoons are commonly found in kitchens. All of these are examples of semantic memory. As we described earlier, long-term memory can be thought of as a semantic network where nodes and links represent the semantic information we have acquired throughout our lives.

Episodic memory is memory for personally experienced life events.[44] So your memory of what you ate for breakfast today is an episodic memory. But your memory of what breakfast is is a semantic memory. Clearly, the two types of memories are related. Semantic memory is built up through our life experience of episodic memories. Still, the two types of memory systems are different. Older adults often report an inability to remember what someone has recently told them (e.g., the name of a new acquaintance) or where they placed their glasses.[45,46] This represents a problem with episodic memories. However, older adults rarely report problems with semantic memories: They know what a name is and what glasses are!

DEVELOPMENTAL ASPECTS OF MEMORY

Working Memory

In general, children's memory improves with age. On tests of memory span (memory for verbal items that must be recalled in their correct serial order), performance increases from two to three items correct at 4 years of age to about six items correct at 12 years of age.[47]

The Phonological Loop

The phonological loop appears to be comprised of two separate subcomponents: the phonological store (used to hold phonological information) and the subvocal rehearsal mechanism (used to keep material alive by repeating the sounds in the phonological store; see an excellent discussion in Gathercole).[48] Subvocal rehearsal does not emerge until about 7 years of age; prior to that age, only the phonological store is available for verbal memory.[49] When words are presented auditorily, the phonological similarity effect and the word length effect (both described earlier) can be demonstrated in children as young as 3 to 5 years of age.[47,50,51,52] Oddly, children of this age don't show these effects when the verbal material is presented visually.[53,54] Instead, they focus on visual aspects of the items rather than trying to recode them into a phonological code (e.g., focusing on visual aspects of pictures rather than converting the pictures into the names of the objects they represent). By approximately age 7, recoding and subvocal rehearsal begins to appear.[55]

The Visuo-Spatial Sketchpad

The visuo-spatial sketchpad also appears to consist of two components: a visual store that holds the physical characteristics of objects, and a spatial mechanism used to plan movements through space and to keep alive the contents of the sketchpad through reactivation (a sort of visual rehearsal). Younger children depend more upon the visuo-spatial sketchpad for remembering visual material than older children (who may engage in recoding into verbal labels for visually presented material and thereby rely upon the phonological loop; see Gathercole[48]). Hitch, Halliday, Schaafstal, and Schraagen found that 5-year-old children were impaired when trying to remember visual material that shared visual features compared to visual material that shared few features.[53] However, 10-year-olds were not impaired by visual similarity. Instead, these older children were impaired by pictures that had lengthy names. This is evidence that the older children were recoding visual information into phonological information and using the phonological loop to rehearse it.

The visual store component increases in size over childhood. Wilson, Scott, and Power used a visual span task in which children were presented with two-dimensional arrays of squares that could be either light or dark.[56] Visual span was measured by slowly increasing the size of the arrays over trials until the child's responses to the query of individual squares were at chance. Visual span, measured in this way, increase from four squares at age 5 to approximately 14 squares at age 11. Eleven-year-old performance was essentially the same as that of adults. Although this increase in span indicates an increase in the visual store, the increase cannot be solely attributed to the visual store. The span task was also performed concurrently with mental arithmetic (which should require the use of both the phonological loop and the central executive), and this decreased span size. This finding indicates that the phonological store and the central executive may also be playing a role in the increase in visual span size with increasing age.

The Central Executive

The central executive is, well, central. It controls the flow of information through working memory, retrieves material from long-term memory when necessary, sets goals for the working memory system, and keeps track of what has been accomplished and what needs doing. One of the ways that working memory is different from the earlier theory of short-term memory is that working memory emphasized both the storage of information and its manipulation. One can think of the central executive as having a certain capacity (which may be different for different individuals). That capacity can be used for either storage of information or processing of information. If the demands of a task require more processing, there's less capacity left for storage and vice versa. Individual differences in working memory capacity strongly predict reasoning ability and fluid intelligence.[57]

One popular measure of complex working memory span (complex because it involves both storage and processing) was developed by Daneman and Carpenter.[58] Individuals either read or listen to sentences and have to process information in the sentences while at the same time remembering the last word of each sentence. The complex working memory span calculated from this task is strongly related to reading comprehension. This complex span also develops throughout childhood. Listening span increases from 1.6 words at age 6 to approximately 6.5 words at age 18.[59] Why does complex memory span increase as children get older? The answer to this is not completely clear, but there are two possibilities. First, it may be that central executive capacity simply increases with age perhaps due to the increasing development of the child's brain. Second, it may be that the operational efficiency of the child's central executive improves due to development and practice. This would mean that more capacity would be left over to handle storage tasks, such as the complex span task previously described. Case et al. found that if operational efficiency differences were held constant, memory span differences across the age spectrum disappeared.[59] The conclusion is that the central executive's abilities improve throughout the school-age years.

Long-Term Memory

As the child grows, so too does the child's store of information in long-term memory. How does this occur? Every day the child has new episodic memories: a visit to the zoo, books read with parents, and interactions at the playground. Gradually these episodic memories develop into semantic memories: The child learns that pandas are bears, that bedtime stories have a typical structure, and that swings require someone to push them. This allows the child to develop interconnections among what were initially isolated facts. Subset and superset category relations are formed as are causal relationships. The end result is an ever more elaborate semantic memory.

This more developed semantic memory allows children to employ memory strategies that were previously not available.[60] Earlier we mentioned that individuals will often recall words from the same category of a list together. Giving an individual the name of a category on a list as a retrieval cue can also improve memory for items from that category.[61] This type of organization in recall can occur only once the child's semantic memory contains the required category relationships among items.

A particularly salient example of this comes from a study by Chi.[62] Earlier research had shown that chess experts were better able to remember the locations of chess pieces on a chessboard than novices (the board position was only briefly presented to participants in the study).[63] But the chess experts could only achieve this memory feat for positions from actual games; when randomly arranged positions were presented, the two groups were equivalent. In Chi's study, she demonstrated that 10-year-old chess experts could outperform novice adults in a chess position memory experiment. Once again, the exceptional performance of the child experts was limited to chess, for which they had a highly developed semantic memory representation. Well-developed semantic memory representations help recall by providing the interconnections that can later be used as retrieval cues. The more ways you have to reach something in long-term memory, the more likely that at least one of those routes will result in a successful recall!

CONCLUSION

The information processing model of human memory comprises three separate memory stores. The first is sensory memory, which holds information for a short period of time in a physical form that is uninterpreted. We attend to some part of sensory memory and move that information into short-term memory. This is where the information is interpreted: It is connected with meaning-based information stored in long-term memory. This process is referred to as pattern recognition. Short-term memory is best explained by the working memory model. Working memory consists of several parts: (a) a central executive that allocates cognitive resources to different aspects of storage and processing and which forms strategies for accomplishing tasks; (b) a phonological loop that handles verbal and phonological material; (c) a visuo-spatial sketchpad that handles visual and spatial material; and (d) an episodic buffer that allows for combining verbal, visual, spatial, and possibly other types of material into realistic percepts of the type our everyday world experiences are made of. Information in working memory can be transferred to long-term memory for more permanent storage. Long-term memory consists of an interconnected semantic network that summarizes our knowledge about things in the world. Long-term memory may also contain episodic memories about our personally lived experiences in the world. Material in long-term memory may be retrieved back into working memory when needed, although the ease of doing so is affected by the retrieval cues available and the organization and structure of long-term memory for the material being retrieved. Together, these three memory stores allow us to experience the world, become experts in the areas we study, and deal with the everyday tasks of teaching and learning.

FURTHER READING

Atkinson, R. C., & Shiffrin, R. M. (1971). The control of short-term memory. *Scientific American*, 225(2), 82–90.

A readable account of the Atkinson–Shiffrin model of short-term memory.

Baddeley, A. D. (1990). *Human memory: Theory and practice*. Needham Heights, MA: Allyn and Bacon.

   Although this is a textbook that covers a lot of information on human memory, it provides a good description of the original Baddeley–Hitch model of working memory. That might come as no surprise, given that it is written by Alan Baddeley.

Gathercole, S. E. (1998). The development of memory. *Journal of Child Psychology and Psychiatry, 39*(1), 3–27.

   An excellent, concise review of memory development in the form of a journal article. It provides a lot of information on the development of working memory.

Gardner, M. K. (2018). The psychology of deep learning. In R. Z. Zheng (Ed.), *Strategies for deep learning with digital technology: Theories and practice in education* (pp. 3–36). New York: Nova Science Publishers.

   This chapter covers a lot of the material reviewed in this chapter although without an emphasis on development. It also contains topics not covered here, such as long-term working memory, the notion of "deliberate practice" in skill building, and the Kintsch–van Dijk construction-integration model of text processing. This is a good place for broadening your understanding of deep learning.

Three

Practical Educational Implications From Research on Memory

Armed with our understanding of the information processing model of memory, we can now consider some practical educational implications with regard to memory. How can we better learn material as students, and how can we better convey material as teachers? We have tried to divide up this material into sections concerning sensory memory, short-term memory (in particular in regard to transferring information into long-term memory), long-term memory, and *metamemory* (which refers to one's own knowledge about one's memory). Occasionally a topic could have been considered under two of these areas, and in these cases the categorization of the topic was based upon our intuitions of where it fits best.

SENSORY MEMORY

Our sensory memory, for the most part, works flawlessly without the need for conscious intervention. Sensory memory holds environmental stimuli briefly until we attend to some portion of it, transfer that information into short-term memory, and connect it with meaning stored in long-term memory. On rare occasions, the process can go awry, as when an ambiguous stimulus is misidentified (e.g., a distant weather balloon is identified as a flying saucer). Recall that information in sensory memory is uninterpreted, and only gross physical features of the store can be differentially attended to. These features (for the visual sensory memory) are things such as space (up versus down and left versus right), color, and, perhaps, motion. For instructors, this means that directing students' attention to the important points of a Power-Point presentation (with regard to sensory memory) involves effective use of space, color, and, possibly, motion. Although these features can grab attention, they should be used sparingly. One needs only think back to poorly designed websites of the 1990s that contained flashing "BUY NOW" signage that constantly changed color. Less is more when directing attention in these particularly salient ways. Perhaps the take-away is that in most situations, sensory memory works well and does not need to be manipulated by teachers.

STRATEGIES FOR TRANSFERRING INFORMATION FROM SHORT-TERM MEMORY TO LONG-TERM MEMORY

Rehearsal

Simple Rehearsal

Rehearsal of verbal material is a way to keep it alive in short-term memory. However, according to Atkinson and Shiffrin, it was also the major mechanism for transferring information from short-term into long-term memory. [2,3] According to these researchers, the longer verbal material was rehearsed, the higher the likelihood it would be stored in long-term memory. Rehearsal can result in material being stored in long-term memory, but it is a relatively primitive method and not particularly reliable. It does not typically make use of meaning, and therefore does not exploit the information already stored in long-term memory. Rehearsal is best suited for relatively meaningless information such as the random digits that make up PIN numbers. When material is meaningless or random, other methods that make use of meaning are not effective, so we may resort to simply rehearsing the material in the hope that it will stick in long-term memory.

As the levels of processing model pointed out, it is not the length of time material is maintained in short-term memory that determines whether we will later remember it (although time plays a role), it is what we do with that material that is critically important.[12] For instance, Jenkins and his associates showed that if participants in an incidental learning experiment (i.e., the participants did not know there would be a later memory test) were induced to perform shallow processing of verbal material (e.g., deciding whether the words were written in upper- or lowercase typeface), the material was poorly recalled.[64,65] If the participants were induced to perform a moderate level of processing (e.g., deciding whether the target word rhymed with another word), later memory was somewhat better. And, finally, if the participants were induced to perform a deep (or semantic) level of processing (e.g., deciding whether the target word would fit into a sentence that was provided: for "house," "The _____ had a front door and many windows"), memory was better still. The point here is that the material remained in short-term memory about the same amount of time in all cases, but later memory for the items was predicted by how the participants processed the information: visually, phonetically, or semantically. Our suggestion is that simple rehearsal should be reserved as a study technique for those stimuli with no inherent semantic characteristics.

Rereading

A learning strategy related to rehearsal is the rereading of textbooks and lecture notes. Rereading is one of the techniques that students most often use when studying for tests.[66,67] Numerous studies have found that rereading can increase recall of information from the reread texts.[68] Why do improvements in memory occur due to rereading? There are two different explanations: the quantitative hypothesis, that rereading increases the total amount of material encoded and transferred to long-term memory (similar to rehearsal), and the qualitative hypothesis, that rereading results in a greater organization of the material into higher-level and lower-level information with greater emphasis given by the learner to the higher-level information.[67] The results of research are mixed but seem to favor the qualitative hypothesis.

Students can reread material repeatedly over short periods of time (massed rereading) or spaced over longer periods of time (spaced rereading). Although both approaches result in improved recall, spaced rereading seems to result in better performance. Also, the question arises as to how many rereadings are necessary to produce good memory for textual material. It appears that the majority of the benefits result from the second reading of material.[67] Beyond that, the law of diminishing returns begins to apply. This is noteworthy because rereading an entire chapter of a college textbook is a time-consuming enterprise. It should be pointed out that most of the research on the benefits of rereading has centered on college students; its applicability to younger students is not well understood. Our recommendation would be that reading can be beneficial with regard to storing material in long-term memory but that it is probably not the most efficient way learners can spend their study time.

Distributed Versus Massed Practice

If we are going to spend an extended period of time studying something, with the hope that we will transfer our knowledge from short-term to long-term memory, then how should we allocate our time? Should we study that thing five times in a row, or should we study it five times but with time in between spent doing something else? The former of these two approaches is referred to as "massed practice"; the latter is referred to as "distributed practice." If our goal is long-term retention, the answer is to follow the distributed practice approach.[67]

The superiority of distributed practice to massed practice has been known for some time. Early paired associate learning studies (learning a list of items of the form A-B, where on testing you will be given the A terms and asked to recall the B terms) showed that there was a definite advantage to having space between repeated presentations of particular A-B pairs.[69] Further, there seemed to be an optimal space between repeated presentations: about eight intervening pairs of other A-B items.[70] Longer spacing was somewhat less effective for memory, as was shorter spacing.

Given that distributed practice produces superior memory performance compared to massed practice, it is interesting that most older students will cram the night before an exam rather than spacing their study over a longer period of time. There are many possible reasons for this behavior. It may be that students are unaware that distributed practice helps learning. It may be that students procrastinate until just before exams and then are forced to rely on massed practice. Finally, it may be that the notion of cramming is passed from one generation of learners to the next: a sort of ignorance begetting ignorance. But, there may be another reason: massed practice often outperforms distributed practice at short retention intervals.[71,72] So if your only goal is to perform well on tomorrow's exam, cramming may work. However, as teachers we seek to encourage learning that passes the test of time, and for that purpose distributed practice is the best approach.

Why does distributed practice benefit learners? There are three possibilities.[67] First, there is the idea of deficient processing. When studying something a second time directly after a first study session, students quickly recognize the material and do not put much effort into encoding it a second time and transferring it to long-term memory. In addition, the feeling of familiarity may lead students to believe they know the material better than they in fact do. Second, there is the possibility that the second presentation of the to-be-learned material at a later time may remind students of the first learning session, causing them to retrieve that learning session. Retrieval practice is a process known to enhance memory. Third, there is the possibility that the second presentation of the to-be-learned material benefits from consolidation of the same material from the first learning session. The longer time between learning sessions in distributed practice leads to greater consolidation, which leads to more benefit during the second learning session. It is not clear which of these possibilities is the reason for distributed practice's superiority; it is possible that all three of them may play some role.

If we wish to distribute our practice over time, what is the best spacing between learning sessions to use? The answer depends upon how long we wish to retain the learning material.[67] In an extensive study by Cepeda, Vul, Rohrer, Wixted, and Pashler,[73] it appears that study sessions work best when the time between them was approximately 10% to 20% of the retention interval. So, if you wish to remember something for 1 year, you'd want to restudy the material every 1.2 to 2.4 months. This has implications for the classroom. Students need to begin studying early in the year if they hope to be able to distribute their learning appropriately (and most students do not do this on their own). Also, teachers need to facilitate distributed learning by reviewing concepts from early classes during later classes, so students' exposure to the material is spaced out over time.[67]

Categorization

In the last chapter, we noted that Bousfield discovered that words on a free recall list that came from the same category tended to be remembered together in recall.[30] The notion of *categorization*, or category members being organized under their superordinate categories, leads to another useful memory strategy: organizing items that fit together under some umbrella so that they may be better recalled at a later point in time. Children as young as second grade judge categorization to be an effective strategy.[74]

To use categorization, the items must of course be able to be organized under category labels. If the learner does not know the category structure of a set of items, the teacher must make clear what the category structures are. Learners without sufficient background knowledge will not be able to use this strategy, so it may be more appropriate for advanced learners rather than novices.

Research on categorization has found that high-frequency members of a category are remembered better than low-frequency members.[75] Further, if one member of a category on a list is remembered, participants in studies will remember about 60% of the members of that category.[76] The mechanism underlying categorization effects could be that individuals use the hierarchical relationships inherent in categories to boost recall, or it could be that the items within a category are simply more highly interrelated than items from a different category (and they, therefore, cue each other). A study that investigated these two possibilities found evidence for both of these mechanisms.[77]

A study of categorized list learning by Tulving and Pearlstone demonstrates just how effective category cues can be in stimulating recall.[26] In one part of their study, the researchers gave two groups of participants a list of 48 words with four items from each of 12 categories. After studying the list, one group of participants was asked to recall as many items as possible, whereas the other group was asked to recall as many items as possible but was given the category names as cues. The "no category name" group recalled about 20 words, whereas the "category name" group recalled about 30 words. After this, the "no category name" group was asked to recall the list again but this time was given the category names as cues. Their recall increased from 20 to 28 words! Clearly the category names allowed the participants to access material in memory that could not otherwise be accessed.

For categorization to work, the category structure must be known at the time of study (when we are attempting to transfer the material from short-term to long-term memory). If we are unaware of the structure, it will do little good later. Sometimes learners can induce the structure when studying by themselves. Categorized items presented together (i.e., blocked) are better remembered than items presented in random order,[61] presumably because learners induce the category structure. With complex material, however, it is incumbent upon the instructor to point out the categorical relationships so that learners may make use of them.

Visual Imagery

Memory for visual material is extremely good. Shepard performed an experiment in which participants viewed 612 pictures and later had to choose which of two presented pictures was the one studied (a forced-choice recognition memory test).[78] Participants' recognition performance was 97% correct immediately after studying the pictures. Over periods of 2 hours, 3 days, and 1 week later, their performance was 100%, 92%, and 87% correct, respectively. It wasn't until 4 months later that their performance dropped to near chance levels (58%). This level of recognition memory is particularly impressive given the large number of items being recalled. The reason that memory for visual material is so good is probably that visual images are relatively distinctive stimuli (compared to words).

The study of visual imagery and memory has mainly centered on specialized memorization techniques or mnemonics. We will discuss three of these in turn: (a) the keyword mnemonic, (b) the method of loci, and (c) the pegword method.

The Keyword Mnemonic

Paired associate learning involves individuals learning lists of items of the form A-B (e.g., house-dog, tree-balloon, wrench-bagel, etc.). At testing, the A terms are presented, and individuals must produce the associated B terms. Bower demonstrated that learning of this type could be enhanced by having individuals form an interacting image of the A and B terms.[79] When the participants in this study were instructed to simply rehearse the pairs, they got approximately 33% correct; when they were instructed to form interacting images of the A and B terms, they got approximately 80% correct! The reason interacting images boost memory performance is twofold: (a) It creates a distinctive representation that is likely to be encoded and not easily confused with other items in memory; and (b) the image has strong associations to both the A and B terms so that when A is presented, it cues the image, which in turn cues the B term (as opposed to other things the A term might be related to).[10]

Raugh and Atkinson converted this idea into the keyword mnemonic for remembering vocabulary in a second language.[80] The foreign language term is associated with an English word that sounds like the foreign word (the keyword). The keyword is then associated with the English translation word by forming an interacting image. At recall, the individual is presented with the foreign language vocabulary item and must produce its English translation. Raugh and Atkinson found that performance for the keyword group was approximately 88% correct compared to approximately 30% for a control group that simply studied the translations: a considerable improvement.

Obviously the keyword mnemonic is not limited to foreign language vocabulary. It can be used in any situation where two items must be remembered together. However, there are some caveats concerning the keyword mnemonic.[67] First, the method works best when the two items to be associated are concrete and can be easily imaged. It's not at all clear what interacting images you would use to recall truth-enterprise. Second, in much of the research, the experimenters have presented the appropriate keywords to participants. The ability of individuals to generate their own keywords likely varies from individual to individual, and younger learners may have particular difficulty in using this mnemonic (both in generating appropriate keywords and in generating the interacting visual images). Third, the benefits from the keyword mnemonic may not last over long retention intervals.[81] At long delays, students may have difficulty decoding the interacting image into its constituent parts, leading to confusion about what the B terms actually are.

In summary, the keyword mnemonic can boost memory for terms that need to be linked. However, it depends on the abilities of students to generate the keywords and images, or it relies on teachers to provide those things to the learner. Because its effects may not be long lasting, booster study sessions should be used to ensure the decoding of the images back into their parts can be performed reliably by students.

The Method of Loci

In ancient Greek times, orators were required to give lengthy speeches in public. Often these speeches involved making several points in a specified serial order. Because paper notes did not exist, orators relied on a visual mnemonic called the method of loci to recall their key points in the correct order.[82] The method consists of three parts.[10] First, the speaker needs to memorize a list of familiar, distinctive places in a familiar order. For instance, one might make a "mental walk" through one's house, focusing on a particular item that is present in each room. Second, for each item on the list to be remembered, the speaker needs to create a vivid image that can easily be associated with each to-be-remembered item. Third, the vivid image for each item is then associated with each familiar place (say the couch in the living room) through the use of an interacting image. When the time comes to recall the information, the speaker retraces the "mental walk," finding each item at each successive place on the walk.

The method of loci is quite successful in boosting serial recall of lists. What the method of loci adds to the keyword method is memory for items in a particular serial order. However, it is subject to some of the same limitations as the keyword mnemonic. It works best when the to-be-remembered items are concrete and easily imaged. Second, the "mental walk" through familiar places must be overlearned for the mnemonic to function efficiently. Third, younger learner may have more difficulty generating the images than older learners. Finally, there is some possibility of interference from previous uses of the mnemonic on current retrieval; that is, one may remember a familiar place with last week's to-be-remembered content rather than today's to-be-remembered content.

The Pegword Method

The pegword method is also a mnemonic for remembering items in a particular serial order. It also relies on interacting visual images to produce its benefits. However, it replaces the memory for a walk through a familiar place with a series of number-word rhymes.[10] So the first step is for the learner to learn the "pegword rhyme": one is a bun, two is a shoe, three is a tree, four is a door, five is a hive, six is sticks, seven is heaven, eight is a gate, nine is a line, and 10 is a hen. Next for each item to be remembered, a distinctive visual image is created. These images are then associated with each item in the pegword rhyme. If I need to remember butter, milk, eggs, and lettuce, I might form images of butter being spread on a bun, a carton of milk being balanced on the toe of a shoe, of eggs hanging as decorations from a tree, and a head of lettuce propping open a door. When I reach the supermarket, I would remember the rhyme, and use the interacting images to retrieve the grocery items in the correct order.

The main difference between the method of loci and the pegword method is that the method of loci requires the learner to produce his or her own set of ordered visual mental cues, whereas the pegword mnemonic provides the visual cues as part of the rhyme. The limitations of the pegword method are essentially the same as those of the method of loci.

Imagery and Text Learning

Given that imagery can enhance memory for lists of items, can imagery support learning for textual material such as school textbooks? The evidence is somewhat mixed on this, but there have been some studies that do show better performance on later testing when students engage in imaging while reading texts.[83] One potential problem is that reading involves utilizing working memory to recode the visual code of printed text into a phonetic code that the articulatory loop can process. This means that the visual code of printed text is competing for resources with the visual imaging of material in the text, which might negatively impact both processes. Research has shown that students who listen to a text and image it perform better than those who read the text and image it.[84,85] However, benefits have been shown for students who read texts. It may be that reading is such an overlearned process that the predicted interference between reading and imaging doesn't have much impact. Also, it should be pointed out that instructing students to image a text may not result in students actually performing the imaging. Denis found that reported use of imagery was significantly correlated with later performance, but instructions to image were not.[86]

Dunlosky, Rawson, Marsh, Nathan, and Willingham review the evidence in support of imaging of texts as an effective method to boost learning and conclude that this technique can improve students' learning.[67] However, they note the benefits of imaging are mostly limited to imagery-friendly materials (e.g., concrete ideas) and that they improve memory for material but not necessarily comprehension. Thus, the technique is most useful when memory is the primary instructional goal.

Verbally Mediated Mnemonics

Whereas the keyword mnemonic, the method of loci, and the pegword mnemonic take advantage of visual imagery, verbally mediated mnemonics take advantage of verbal elaboration and chunking. The to-be-remembered items are linked together into a larger coherent verbal structure such as a sentence, where the first letters of each word are cues for the to-be-remembered items. Because a sentence is an integrated unit, more words can be remembered in the context of a sentence than could be remembered in isolation. Some examples will make the method clear.

Students who learn to read the musical staff are often taught the sentence "Every good boy deserves fudge." Here, the first letters of the words give the musical notes of the lines of the staff: E, G B, D, and F (from highest to lowest note). In this use of verbal mediation, the first letters are the to-be-remembered items, and no further cueing is necessary.

A slightly more complicated verbal application involves the cranial nerves. Anatomy students are often taught the sentence "On old Olympus's towering top a Finn and German viewed some hops." Here the first letters of the sentence serve as cues for the cranial nerves in order from first through 12th: (a) O: olfactory nerve; (b) O: optic nerve; (c) O: oculomotor nerve; (d) T: trochlear nerve; (e) T: trigeminal nerve; (f) A: abducens nerve; (g) F: facial nerve; (h) A: auditory nerve; (i) G: glossopharyngeal nerve; (j): V: vagus nerve; (k) S: spinal accessory nerve; and (l) H: hypoglossal nerve. The sentence also benefits from rhyming as it is usually spoken as a rhyming couplet.

One of us taught students about Hermann Ebbinghaus in a class on cognitive psychology. The important points to remember were that Ebbinghaus developed **O**bjective **M**ethods to study memory, including the **R**elearning **M**ethod and the **S**avings **S**core, that he used **C**alibrated **U**nits which were **N**onsense **S**yllables, and that he studied **R**emote **A**ssociation and used **S**tatistical **M**ethods. This is obviously a lot of material to remember, especially if you don't have previous knowledge about Hermann Ebbinghaus. To help students with the task, they were taught the following sentence: "On Montana ranches, milking smelly spotted cows until night seems routine and sometimes mundane." The sentence was paired with a parsing rule: separate the first letters into pairs. This leads to the following: (a) OM, (b) RM, (c) SS, (d) CU, (e) NS, (f) RA, and (d) SM. These letters then serve as cues to remember the specific facts about Ebbinghaus. Of course, one still needs to have the information in memory, but the retrieval cues make the process of getting the information out of memory much simpler. This application of verbally mediated mnemonics adds the parsing rule to the use of sentences.

Commonsense Methods

There are a couple of learning methods pursued by students without explicit instruction. Dunlosky, Rawson, Marsh, Nathan, and Willingham provide an excellent review of these, which we will summarize here. We discussed rereading of texts earlier.[67] Next we discuss highlighting or underlining of texts and summarization of texts.

Highlighting or Underlining

When asked about their study techniques, students commonly report highlighting or underling important information in their textbooks.[87,88] The idea is simple enough: Highlighting important information makes it stand out, and it is easier to find during later studying. This should facilitate transfer from short-term to long-term memory. Unfortunately, the research has not necessarily supported the notion of better learning through highlighting and underlining. A study by Fowler and Barker found that groups that highlighted text or read text highlighted by others did not outperform a control group that simply read the text.[89] It may be that students who highlight have difficulty discriminating the most important ideas in the texts they read. Another problem is that students tend to over highlight. Fowler and Barker found a negative correlation between the amount of material highlighted and later test performance in their study. Thus highlighting and underlining, as it is typically used by students, does not increase memory for important material.

Summarization

Teachers often ask students to write summarizations of texts in an effort to help them focus on what is important or determine how different ideas connect to one another. The underlying mechanism for summarization supporting learning is that the summary process forces learners to organize material to be remembered. Instead of a string of equally important sentences in the original text, the learner is compelled to develop a (potentially hierarchical) structure in which important ideas are emphasized over less important details. Research has supported the fact that summarization can enhance learning.[90] However, students are not necessarily good at producing good summaries without explicit instruction and practice. Dunlosky, Rawson, Marsh, Nathan, and Willingham point out that "higher quality summaries that contained more information and that were linked to prior knowledge were associated with better performance" (p. 15).[67] Summarization can enhance memory and learning over periods of days and weeks. The real question in using summarization in the classroom is whether students have the ability to produce high-quality summaries and whether they have the background knowledge that is prerequisite. Older learners are more likely to have these characteristics than younger learners, so the technique may work best with later high school and college students.

RETRIEVING INFORMATION FOR LONG-TERM MEMORY

Once information has been stored in long-term memory, learners need to be able to retrieve that information for later use or testing. This is the point at which accessing information becomes crucial. Access to stored information occurs via retrieval cues.

A retrieval cue is a word, image, or idea that sparks another item in long-term memory and allows it to be moved from long-term back to short-term memory. Critically, the cue must have been associated with the stored information at some earlier point in time, usually during encoding of the information. Tulving and Osler provided a critical study in this regard.[91] They had participants study 24 words either in the presence of a weak associate of the word (this was to be the retrieval cue) or in the absence of the weak associate. Then, at test, half of the participants received the weak associate as a cue and half received no retrieval cue. The results showed that the weak associate retrieval cue aided recall but only if it had been present at study with the to-be-remembered item. What mattered was that the cue was associated with the item to be recalled during study and present at recall. Tulving and Thomson generalized this finding into the *encoding specific principle*: Only information stored at the time an item is studied can serve as a retrieval cue.[92]

Retrieval cues can be explicit, as in the Tulving and Osler study, or they can be implicit, as in the context occurring at the time a list is studied. An interesting example of this comes from a study by Godden and Flavell.[93] Divers learned a list of words either on the shore or 20 feet underwater. They were then tested either on the shore or underwater. Recall was best when the study context matched the testing context: Words learned underwater were better recalled when tested underwater, and words learned on shore were better recalled when tested on shore. The influences of context can also be seen in the effects of mood on memory. Bower and colleagues demonstrated that happy people are better at remembering happy events, whereas sad people are better at remembering sad events.[94,95,96] These findings lead to an interesting instructional application: Students will do best on tests when they study in the room where the test will be given. In this case the room itself will serve as a contextual retrieval cue.

One of the most important things students can do while learning new material is to connect that material to information already in long-term memory. This helps organize the new material, and it provides multiple retrieval cues to access that new material later in time. Information that is stored as isolated bits of knowledge cannot be integrated into larger wholes that provide meaning and allow students to make inferences.

Elaborative Interrogation

Elaborative interrogation involves asking students to answer "Why?" questions about new information to be learned.[97] This technique has been shown to facilitate learning. Dunlosky, Rawson, Marsh, Nathan, and Willingham state that elaborative interrogation has its effect through enhancing the integration of new information with existing information already in long-term memory.[67] For instance, if students learn that they would weigh less on the moon, they might ask themselves, "Why would I weigh less on the moon? What would cause that to occur?" This might lead the student to connect weight with the size of the gravitational field exerted by a planet. Elaborative interrogation also facilitates learning by helping students discover the similarities and differences between new and prior knowledge (through prompts that either explicitly or implicitly encourage students to compare and contrast information).

The amount of prior knowledge that learners have is an important determinant of the effectiveness of elaborative interrogation.[67] The more information a learner already has about a topic, the greater the benefits from elaborative interrogation. Basically, without relevant organized knowledge structures in long-term memory, it is difficult for the learner to integrate the new information. It is these knowledge structures that provide the retrieval cues for later recall and the structure for comparing and contrasting new information to prior knowledge.

Schemata and Knowledge Structures

We should say a bit more about schemata and knowledge structures. The notion of schemas dates back to Piaget.[60] For Piaget, a scheme was a qualitative way in which the child interacted with the world. Thus the schema was a large-scale knowledge structure. Later researchers in computer science used the notion of a frame or script, which was also a knowledge structure, to help computers understand text.[98,99] Much of what we know is not explicitly stated in what we read. To use an example from Schank and Abelson, if you read a story about lunch in a restaurant, but it is not stated that the customer paid his or her bill after eating, you can assume it is true because of your "restaurant script." If for some reason the customer actually hadn't paid the bill, it would have been stated in the story because note would need to be made of this aberration. Our schemas allow us to fill in the missing details when reading texts about stereotypic situations. As we learn more about academic subjects, we develop mental structures about these areas as well. When reading new material, we should attempt to attach it to our existing schemas so that we may make inferences when asked transfer questions and so that we have additional retrieval routes for recall.

Recall itself is a reconstructive process. We remember many details, but when a detail is missing, we use our knowledge structures to "fill in the gaps." Usually this processes aids us, but occasionally it can lead us in the wrong direction. A classic study was performed by Bartlett.[100] He had participants, who were all English university students, listen to and later recall a story based upon Pacific Northwest Indian culture titled "The War of the Ghosts." The actual story involved many things that would be outside of everyday English culture: traveling in canoes, war parties, spirits who were ghosts, and something black coming out of the mouth of an Indian who was struck in battle. When the recall protocols of the English students were analyzed, it appeared that many details were left out, and in their place new details were created that were more consistent with English culture. Thus, the English cultural schema was used to aid in recall of the story, but it was inappropriate due to the fact that the story came from a different culture with a different schema. The point here is that knowledge structures can aid recall but only if the appropriate knowledge structures are activated at the time of recall.

Practice Testing

Practice testing material that we later need to retrieve from long-term memory enhances learning.[67,101,102,103] There appears to be two reasons why practice testing aids in recall: (a) direct effects and (b) mediated effects. As to direct effects, it seems that attempting to recall something newly learned activates related information in memory. This information is then encoded with the to-be-retrieved information, and the related information provides additional retrieval paths to access the new information. As to mediated effects, practice testing facilitates the elaboration of the to-be-retrieved information, and these elaborations also serve as retrieval cues at recall.[104,105] Practice testing may also help students organize the to-be-retrieved information, which should also benefit recall.[106,107]

In their review of practice testing effects, Dunlosky, Rawson, Marsh, Nathan, and Willingham note several things that improve the effects of practice testing.[67] First, practice tests that require the learner to generate a response outperform practice tests that simply require filling in a blank or recognizing previously studied material. Second, more practice tests are better than fewer practice tests. Third, spacing practice tests over time is better than massed practice tests, and longer spacing intervals are better than shorter spacing intervals. Finally, practice testing with feedback about what the correct response was outperforms practice testing without feedback. Practice testing is superior to simply restudying the material. In conclusion, practice testing material you will later need to recall is an effective means of ensuring later memory, and it can be used for widely varying types of material.

Self-Explanation

When performing a complex task, or when dealing with new complex material, it is advantageous to have learners self-explain what they are doing to themselves.[67] Self-explanation can support memory by integrating new information with existing knowledge structures, just as elaborative interrogation. These knowledge structures then provide additional retrieval routes to the to-be-learned material.

Self-explanation effects can be found in both younger and older learners, and it is applicable across many types of learning materials (e.g., logic puzzles, math problems, and learning from text). One issue, though, with self-explanation is that students need to be able to produce adequate self-explanations for the method to produce superior learning. There is a positive relationship between the quantity and quality of self-explanations that students produce and later test performance. This implies that students must already possess the requisite knowledge structures needed and the ability to produce self-explanations. If they do not, they may be aided by explicit instruction in self-explanation (along with providing the necessary background knowledge).[108,109]

METAMEMORY

As adults, we are aware of a number of things about memory and our capacity to remember material in any particular context. We know that memory isn't perfect and that some tasks will require more effort to correctly perform them than others. We know that there are limits to our memory. We also know that we can perform certain activities (rehearsal, imaging, elaborating, self-explanation, and particular mnemonic methods) to enhance our memory. This knowledge of memory as an area of mental competence, and our skills and limitations within it, is referred to as "metamemory."

Metamemory develops as children age (see Flavell, Miller, and Miller for an excellent discussion).[60] For instance, we have spoken of retrieval cues: information that leads us to a piece of information we need to recall. Researchers have pointed out that "cognitive cueing" is a concept that children gradually acquire.[93,110] Young children may not understand this basic cognitive concept. For instance, in a study where children needed to remember under which of four identical cups a penny had been hidden, 40% of 4- and 5-year-olds thought that hiding a paperclip (which was to cue the correct cup) under the opaque cup would serve as a good cue for later memory!

The most basic kind of metamemory knowledge concerns the basic ideas of remembering and forgetting.[60] These ideas begin to form during the early preschool years. Further, older children have a better sense of what they can remember than younger children. In a study by Flavell, Friedrichs, and Hoyt, children were shown a set of pictures of common objects.[111] On each trial, the children were asked whether they could remember the series or if it had gotten too long to remember. With each trial, the series size increased by one. Kindergarteners often thought they could remember 10 pictures, whereas their actual memory span was closer to four pictures. But as children's age increased, their predicted span more closely approximately their actual span. Whereas, in general, young children overestimate their span, in some cases they underestimate it. When shown a list of categorizable items, there is a tendency for younger children to underestimate, presumably because they do not understand how categorization can boost one's memory.[112]

Children's knowledge of the difficulty of memory tasks also improves with age.[60] Young children recognize that the number of items on a memory list increases task difficulty.[113] When asked to generate three words that would be easy to recall along with "blue," older elementary school children are more likely to generate three other colors than younger elementary school children.[114] Likewise, older children are more likely than younger children to understand that remembering a list of words will be harder if they are required to learn a second list of words prior to testing (a phenomenon known in the memory literature as retroactive interference).[115]

Children also develop the memory strategies we discussed earlier as they age. One might wonder why younger children, whose memories seem most in need of support, don't use effective strategies. There are multiple reasons. First, they may never have come across the strategy and therefore don't know of its existence. Second, even when they know of a strategy, they may not be able to employ it effectively. Children possess a certain amount of working memory capacity. This capacity either increases with age, or the efficiency with which it can be used increases with age, or both. The use of memory strategy consumes some of this capacity, and it consumes more capacity if the strategy is new and not automated. For the younger child, the cognitive demands of using a strategy may outweigh its benefits. If almost all of working memory is necessary to utilize the strategy, then there may be insufficient memory left over to maintain the to-be-remembered items.

But as the child becomes older, the efficiency of working memory increases, and the strategy becomes more practiced and automatic. At this point the child can use the strategy to good effect to boost recall.

As our metamemory improves, our ability to identify and solve memory tasks improves. Even as adults, we are still learning new memory strategies (perhaps you've picked up a few from this chapter). Improvement in our metamemory makes us more strategic learners who are better equipped to deal with the demands of the classroom. Teachers can aid students by making them aware of effective memory strategies and by scaffolding these strategies while students are still in the process of automating them.

CONCLUSION

Our knowledge of the information processing system leads to suggestions about how to better remember material we are trying to learn. For the most part, sensory memory works efficiently and is not amenable to interventions. The majority of our practical advice relates to the following two aspects of memory: (a) moving material from short-term (or working) to long-term memory and (b) retrieving information in long-term memory. The dichotomy is somewhat artificial as the best techniques involve both storage and retrieval.

Rehearsal is one technique for moving material to long-term memory, but it is one of the least effective. It is best for material that has no meaningful structure inherent in the information to be stored (e.g., personal identification numbers). When studying material, there is a clear advantage for spaced, rather than massed, practice. Massed practice may get you through tomorrow's exam, but for longer-term learning one needs to space one's studying over time. If the material you are learning involves a categorical structure, you can make use of this structure to prompt your memory during later recall. We discussed three imagery-based mnemonic techniques (the keyword mnemonic, the method of loci, and the pegword method) that can all be used to improve later recall. These are especially useful when you need to recall items from cues, such as when learning foreign language vocabulary or remembering the points in a talk in the order you wish to present them. We also learned that imaging text during study can boost later memory for that textual material. There are also mnemonics based on verbal mediation or elaboration in which the learner turns the first letter of each to-be-remembered item into the first letter of words of an easily memorable sentence. This mnemonic is supported in part by chunking: turning isolated bits of information into a smaller number of larger-scale units that don't exceed the limits on working memory.

Students engage in some study techniques such as highlighting and summarization that have mixed benefits. Highlighting is not particularly effective as students often highlight too much and do not organize material into more and less important categories. Summarization can benefit learning, but students need the requisite background knowledge and may need instruction in producing good summaries.

When retrieving information from long-term memory, it is necessary that the retrieval cues used to access the material have been associated with the to-be-learned material at study. The more retrieval cues, the better, and techniques such as elaborative interrogation, practice testing, and self-explanation increase the number of cues available to learners. The techniques benefit from integrating new material with existing knowledge structures. Such integration also allows students to better answer inference questions and to grow their schemas into more complex and differentiated knowledge structures (rather than allowing knowledge to exist as isolated islands). Practice testing also benefits from distributed practice of to-be-learned material.

Metamemory, which is our knowledge about our own memory, memory tasks, and memory strategies, increases with age. As our knowledge of our own memory abilities improves, we can approach learning and memory tasks more strategically. Mnemonic strategies become better practiced and automated with increasing age and usage. This allows us to succeed in the all-important task of storing and retrieving information from long-term memory.

FURTHER READING

Dunlosky, J., Rawson, K. A., Marsh, E. J., Nathan, M. J., & Willingham, D. T. (2013). Improving students' learning with effective learning techniques: Promising directions from cognitive and educational psychology. *Psychological Science in the Public Interest*, 14(1), 4–58.

> This excellent review covers 10 techniques commonly used to improve classroom learning. The research underlying each technique is covered as well as an overall evaluation of each. This review is both easily readable and directly relevant to students and teachers.

Flavell, J. H., Miller, P. H., & Miller, S. A. (1993). *Cognitive development* (3rd ed.). Englewood Cliffs, NJ: Prentice Hall.

> This textbook on cognitive development reviews the development of memory and metamemory among other topics. It is aimed at intermediate level college students and is quite understandable.

Schneider, W., & Pressley, M. (1997). *Memory development between two and twenty* (2nd ed.). Mahwah, NJ: Lawrence Erlbaum Associates.

> This is a more advanced book on the development of memory during childhood and adolescence. This book delves more deeply into the research and is written at a graduate student level. Still, if you want to see a review of the original research in the field, this is a good place to start.

Glass, A. L., & Holyoak, K. J. (1986). *Cognition* (2nd ed.). New York: Random House.

This book is a textbook on cognitive psychology and provides a good description of mnemonics, retrieval cues, and reconstructive recall. It is written at the undergraduate level and would be easily readable by most college students.

Four

Working Memory, Cognitive Load, and Learning

In Chapter Two we discussed types of memory including sensory memory, short-term memory (also known as working memory, although some cognitive scientists point out the differences between the two), and long-term memory. We also described the path of information encoding in which the information from sensory memory gets encoded in short-term memory to make sense of new information. Some of the information in short-term memory later gets encoded into long-term memory to become part of our schemas. It is evident working or short-term memory (for the convenience of discussion, we hereto after use the term "working memory" instead of "short-term memory" in this chapter) plays a key role in organizing sensory information into meaningful semantic units and entering the semantic units into long-term memory. In that regard, understanding the role of working memory and the resources in working memory associated with learning is critical to teachers who would like to design instructions that support students' cognitive and affective learning in classrooms.

We mentioned that working memory is limited both in duration and capacity. Studies have shown that working memory can store about seven plus or minus one elements but normally operates on only two or three elements.[6,116] When working memory becomes overloaded with information, learning can be adversely affected. For example, a learner becomes cognitively overwhelmed when (a) the content is too complex and (b) there is no relevant schema in the domain. Besides the content complexity and a lack of schemas in learning, learners' cognitive overload can be induced by improper design in instruction causing unnecessary cognitive processes in working memory. Sweller and associates studied the relationship between types of cognitive load and the context in which the cognitive load is induced.[117,118,119] They identified three types of cognitive load that are believed to directly impact the performance of working memory. The three types of cognitive load include intrinsic, extraneous, and germane cognitive load. The next section reviews the types of cognitive load and the context in which the cognitive load is induced.

TYPES OF COGNITIVE LOAD

Intrinsic Cognitive Load

Intrinsic cognitive load is induced by the complexity of the content. It refers to the mental load imposed upon the learner's working memory caused by overly complex materials. The level or the degree of intrinsic cognitive load is defined by the element interactivity in the learning content. Element interactivity is described as a state in which elements in the learning content interact with each other. High element interactivity indicates a high level of content difficulty.

Element interactivity varies in degree and intensity based on how many elements interact with each other at one time. For example, the element interactivity in memorizing the vocabulary words like "car," "road," and "run" is relatively low because the learner does not need to know how the words are related and what they mean to each other. In other words, the words can be learned independently by the learner without understanding whether and how the individual words are related to each other. However, the element interactivity increases when the learner is reading a sentence like "a car is running on the road," in which three words interact and rely on each other to form a meaningful message.

In processing the sentence the reader needs to understand the structure of the sentence, the verb tenses, the meanings of the words, and their parts of speech. For example, the learner has to consider the subject–verb agreement when reading the sentence. Obviously, the reading process involving "a car is running on the road" has higher element interactivity than that of memorizing three words independently. High element interactivity indicates the level of difficulty for the content is high, which also means the learner will have a high intrinsic cognitive load when processing the content.

To further illustrate the degree and the intensity of the element interactivity, the following presents two examples involving mathematical problem-solving. The problem on the left involves two digits (3 and 5) with a two-step procedure: (a) adding 3 to 5 and (b) calculating the result within the range of 10 (no carryover). The problem on the right has four digits (5, 6, 4, and 7) with eight steps involving multiple carryovers:

(1) Add 6 to 7
(2) Calculate the result.
(3) Add 1 carryover to 10th position.
(4) Add 5 to 4.
(5) Calculate the result.
(6) Add carryover 1.

(7) Calculate the result.
(8) Add 1 carryover to 100th position.

$$
\begin{array}{r}
3 \\
+\ 5 \\
\hline
8
\end{array}
\qquad
\begin{array}{r}
{}^{1}5\ {}^{1}6 \\
+\ 4\quad 7 \\
\hline
1\ 0\ 3
\end{array}
$$

Figure 4.0 Math Problems

It is evident that the problem on the right is more complex and cognitively demanding due to a high level of element interactivity compared to the problem on the left. In any learning situation, high element interactivity indicates a high level of difficulty content and thereby is cognitively more demanding and requires more mental effort in learning.

It should be noted that the element interactivity and content difficulty level are relative to individuals' prior knowledge. A mathematics problem that is difficult for a novice learner may be less challenging for an experienced learner who usually has meaningful knowledge units stored in his or her long-term memory. For example, in solving a mathematics problem like $(5 - 2) \times (6 - 3)$, the experienced learner probably treats the elements in the parentheses $(5 - 2)$ and $(6 - 3)$ as single units that reduce element interactivity. As such, the experienced learner can proceed directly to the solution step of $3 \times 3 = 9$. In contrast, the novice learner has to first find the results of $(5 - 2)$ and $(6 - 3)$ and then moves onto the step of $3 \times 3 = 9$. Without a relevant schema, the element interactivity for the novice learner is high, whereas the experienced learner may find the element interactivity low because he or she already has the schema to integrate new information in learning.

The relation between element interactivity and expertise can be best understood in the example of music sight-reading. A concert master can sight-read and play the music simultaneously. The measures in the music, for example, are being processed in chunks without going into detail about what the type of clef, the length of notes, and the tempo are. For the concert master, the knowledge is retrieved from his or her schema and automatically applied to music sight-reading almost unconsciously. The element interactivity for the concert master is thus low. Such a process can be different for a novice violin player.

The novice player does not have an adequate schema to process the music; he or she has to treat every element separately. That is, he or she will process the music at every detail by identifying the type of clef, determining the length of notes (half, quarter, eighth, or 16th), figuring out the beat and tempo, and so forth. The element interactivity for the novice player processing the music is high. Consequently, the novice player will find the music sight-reading more difficult and is likely to experience higher cognitive load than will the concert master.

Teachers who develop their instructions to improve students' learning should become aware of the role of element interactivity in students' cognitive processing. It is also recommended that teachers pay attention to the interaction between element interactivity and expertise so their instructions are designed in ways that best support low and high prior-knowledge learners in terms of cognitive load management in learning.

Extraneous Cognitive Load

Extraneous cognitive load refers to the mental load caused by improper design in instruction. For example, information that is redundant to learning unnecessarily taxes the working memory resources and thus imposes extraneous cognitive load on the learner. Although there are many factors contributing to ineffectiveness in learning, poorly designed instructions causing redundancy and split attention impose extraneous cognitive load on the learners, making cognitive resources in working memory less available for learning.

Redundancy in Learning

Redundancy describes a phenomenon in learning in which the learner spends additional mental effort to process (a) redundant information that he or she has already known or (b) repetitive content through multiple sensory inputs.

Information Redundancy

Learning becomes redundant when additional information is unwittingly added to the instruction by the teacher who is unaware that the information may be redundant to some learners. For example, when teaching the distributive law in a mathematics class, the teacher is not aware that some of the students had a summer math camp and therefore know the content. To ensure that the students have adequate support while learning the content, the teacher includes the definitions for the subtypes of distributive law (associative and commutative laws; see Figure 4.1 Example A). This creates a redundancy for students who attended the math camp in summer. By processing the redundant definitions, the learner who has the prior knowledge through the summer camp may experience extraneous cognitive load. He or she has to spend extra effort in going through the redundant information, which is a waste of cognitive resources and imposes unnecessary mental load on the learner.

Redundant Multimodal Presentation

Another form of redundancy is presenting the content through multiple sensory inputs. Figure 4.1 Example B presents an example of improper design in instruction. The content is related to studying the combustion system of a car engine with multimedia. The learner watches an animation that shows how the combustion system of a car engine works, listens to the process depicting the combustion system, and reads the on-screen text that is identical to the narrative description. The design of instruction raises some concerns with regard to learners' cognitive information processing. It

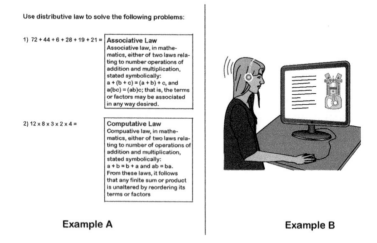

Example A   **Example B**

Figure 4.1 Examples of Redundancy Design

dictates the learner attend to the on-screen text and the animation simultaneously while listening to the narration. This can be a problem for the learner. First, because the animation and on-screen text are both visuals, they can compete with each other for the cognitive resources in visual memory. The result is the learner will miss learning information in either the animation or the on-screen text. Next, because the on-screen text is identical to the information in narration, reading the on-screen text while listening to the same information requires extra mental effort to process the redundant information, which can be a drain on cognitive resources in working memory. It is apparent that more mental effort is required to process the narrated content (auditory) while attending to on-screen text and animation (visual). By processing the three sources of information at the same time, the learner is likely to experience a high extraneous cognitive load.

There is research to support the design of instruction for reducing the extraneous cognitive load caused by redundant multimodal presentation.[120,121] Mayer and associates investigated the differences between two types of instructional design in multimedia learning: narration+animation and narration+animation+identical on-screen text. They found that learners who learned with narration+animation outperformed these who learned with narration+animation+identical on-screen text as measured by recall and transfer. Mayer and associates explained that the narration+animation+identical on-screen text design caused the cognitive resources in working memory to become less available with redundant information in visual memory. The learners had a hard time generating mental representations of the new information as they constantly switched between animation and on-screen text. In contrast, the narration+animation design eliminated the redundancy effect. The learners are able to cross-reference the information from narration and animation to form mental representations of the new learning content.

Teachers who are interested in integrating multimedia in their teaching should be cognizant of the cognitive functions of different media and their roles in learners' information processing. Improper design in instruction can cause extraneous cognitive load and impede learning.

Learner Expertise

Like intrinsic cognitive load, extraneous cognitive load is relative to individual learners' expertise. For experienced learners, the poorly designed instruction has little effect on their learning because the experienced learners who already have the schemas will learn the content regardless of the design. Sweller explains that the content element interactivity for experienced learners is low, therefore the format of content presentation has little impact on their learning. In contrast, poorly designed instruction can pose a challenge to novice learners for the following reasons.[122] First, the novice learner who lacks a schema in the relevant domain often finds him- or herself facing high element interactivity in the learning material. That is, the novice learner has already encountered a strain of cognitive resources in working memory due to intrinsic cognitive load induced by high element interactivity. Second, with poorly designed instruction, such as redundant information, the novice learner has to spend extra cognitive resources to deal with the poor design, which will lead to a cognitive overload. In situations where both intrinsic and extraneous cognitive load are high, the novice learners are less likely to succeed in learning.

Split Attention in Learning

Split attention is another example of improper design that induces extraneous cognitive load in learning. It refers to the cognitive process in which the learner divides his or her attention between two corresponding sources of information in learning. Figure 4.2 presents the examples of split attention. Example A describes the combustion system of a car engine. The instructional material contains a picture, a list of glossary terms, and numbers in the picture corresponding to the terms of the glossary. To understand how the combustion system works, the learner studies the parts of combustion system by splitting his or her attention between the numbers in the picture and their corresponding terms in the glossary list. The process of switching between the picture and glossary causes a split attention, imposing extraneous cognitive load on the learner as he or she coordinates two sources of information to make sense of the learning material.

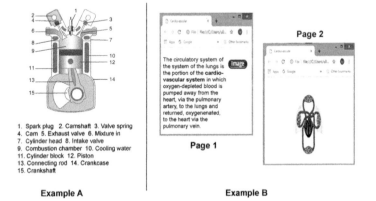

1. Spark plug 2. Camshaft 3. Valve spring
4. Cam 5. Exhaust valve 6. Mixture in
7. Cylinder head 8. Intake valve
9. Combustion chamber 10. Cooling water
11. Cylinder block 12. Piston
13. Connecting rod 14. Crankcase
15. Crankshaft

Example A

Example B

Figure 4.2 Example of Split-Attention Design

Similarly, the design of Example B splits learners' attention between the text and image pages, resulting in high extraneous cognitive load. The text page contains information about the cardiovascular system. It describes how the cardiovascular system works in terms of providing fresh blood to the body. The image page contains an image demonstrating visually the cardiovascular system, which corresponds to the information on the text page. Consider the situation in which the learner tries to learn left and right atriums in the heart. The learner first reads the text information about left and right atriums on the text page. Next, he or she clicks the image page to study the positions of left and right atriums and their relations with different blood vessels. To understand the function of the atriums, the learner has to hold in working memory the information from the text page while moving to the image page to study their shapes, positions, and relation to vessels. The act of switching between the pages splits the learner's attention between the text and image pages, while the working memory must coordinate the information from the two separated sources. The result is the learner will have a high extraneous cognitive load with poor performance in learning.

Germane Cognitive Load

In addition to intrinsic and extraneous cognitive loads, germane cognitive load is the third type of cognitive load that plays a key role in learners' cognitive information processing. Germane cognitive load refers to the mental load induced in learning to construct new knowledge or build a new schema.[119] Unlike extraneous cognitive load, which impedes the learner's learning, germane cognitive load is relevant to learning. Germane cognitive load is related to learners' motivation in learning and associated with intrinsic cognitive load.[122]

Relation to Intrinsic Cognitive Load

Germane cognitive load is a type of cognitive load devoted to the construction of new knowledge and schemas. For germane cognitive load to occur, the content must be difficult enough so the learner feels challenged.[123] That is, by placing him or her in the zone of proximal development (ZPD), the learner starts to experience some level of pressure from the content that shows a moderate or higher level of element interactivity. The level of cognitive pressure or challenge that reflects intrinsic cognitive load in learning incentivizes the learner to become engaged in learning.

Designing instruction based on Vygotsky's ZPD theory can be beneficial to learners' learning. When the instruction is taught in the ZPD, learners are more motivated and interested to learn something new and challenging. The question is how to design instruction in which intrinsic cognitive load is manipulated to induce germane cognitive load to support learners' schema construction. One possible answer is to lower the element interactivity of the content by taking into consideration learners' prior knowledge so the content is challenging but not cognitively overwhelming. Understanding the relationship between germane cognitive load and instructional design benefits teachers to design and develop instruction that induces learners' germane cognitive load to engage in meaningful and sustained effort in knowledge acquisition.

Relation to Motivation

As discussed previously, germane cognitive load is related to learners' motivation. Evidence has shown that germane cognitive load is significantly correlated with multiple motivation measures such as persistence and interest.[124,125] Instructional materials that are characterized with cognitive pressure (e.g., difficult content, element interactivity, etc.) are likely to motivate learners to learn. For example, a second grader may have little motivation to learn single-digit addition if he or she already knows how to do this mathematic operation. By increasing the difficulty level, say multiple-digit addition, the learner comes out of his or her comfort zone and feels cognitively challenged. He or she is then motivated and ready to spend effort to learn something new. We see here an increase of germane cognitive load related to knowledge construction and learning.

LEVERAGING WORKING MEMORY RESOURCES FOR LEARNING

As an active memory storage, working memory holds transient information with a limited processing capacity. The capacity of working memory reflects a negative relationship between the cognitive resources and intrinsic and extraneous cognitive load. The higher the intrinsic and extraneous cognitive load, the fewer the cognitive resources will be available in working memory. Fewer cognitive resources lead to worse performance in tasks that require working memory. Therefore, managing cognitive load in the design and development of instruction has significant implications in teaching and learning.

Managing Intrinsic and Extraneous Cognitive Load in Learning

If the content is difficult, meaning the element interactivity and intrinsic cognitive load are high, the design of the instructional materials must be optimized to lower the extraneous cognitive load. Otherwise, there will not be enough cognitive resources in the working memory to process the content. On the contrary, if the extraneous cognitive load is high due to an improper design of instruction, the intrinsic cognitive load must be low. That is, the content element inter-activity should be controlled at the level that is within the learner's comfort zone to process the material. Low element interactivity allows the learner to handle the learning content regardless of the design of instruction.

Relationship among Intrinsic, Extraneous, and Germane Cognitive Load

Germane cognitive load, which is related to schema con-struction, is positively correlated with intrinsic cognitive load and negatively correlated with extraneous cognitive load. As mentioned previously, germane cognitive load is induced by intrinsic cognitive load, provided the intrinsic cognitive load does not overly tax the cognitive resources in working memory. For effective learning to occur, the content must be complex enough to create a ZPD in which the learner feels challenged and becomes motivated to spend the effort to learn the material.

The positive relationship between the content and learner effort suggests the content should be designed in such a way that the complexity of the content warrants the learner's effort to engage in meaningful learning. However, the positive relationship between intrinsic and germane cognitive load is based on the assumption that the extraneous cognitive load must be low. In other words, the instruction must be prop-erly designed to minimize the irrelevant cognitive process-ing (e.g., redundancy or split attention) to allow the working memory system to have sufficient cognitive resources for complex learning.

Instructional Strategies Based on Working Memory Resources

The question of how learners can learn best given the limited cognitive resources in working memory has become a pressing issue for educators, parents, and policy makers. Although efforts have been made to develop types of instructional strategies (e.g., domain general vs. domain specific, cognitive vs. metacognitive, surface vs. deep, etc.) in support of instructional practice and student learning,[126] instructional strategies that take into account the learner's cognitive load, their limited cognitive resources in working memory, and the subsequent impact they have on learning are still underdeveloped.

Instructional strategies focusing on cognitive load and working memory resources begin to show promise in content learning, cognitive processing, and outcomes related to deep and surface learning. For example, instructional strategies like pretraining and worked examples are used to help build learners' schemas to lower the element interactivity and intrinsic cognitive load so more cognitive resources become available during learning.

Although some strategies focus on reducing intrinsic cognitive load by building learner schemas, others attend to the design of instruction to optimize the cognitive resources in working memory by minimizing extraneous cognitive load. Figure 4.3 describes a spatial-related learning scenario in which the learners are asked to solve a geometry problem by finding the value of one of the angles in a triangle given the values of other two angles. Two instructional strategies are developed to present the same information. One strategy uses two separate web pages to present the text and diagram information respectively (Example A). The other includes the

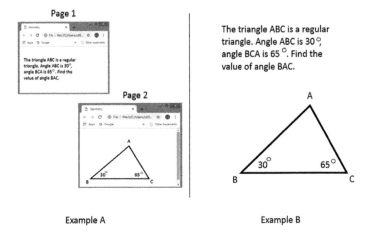

Figure 4.3 Instructional Strategies for Spatial-Related Learning

text and diagram in a single page (Example B). Which instructional strategy would help learners learn better?

Based on the discussion relating to split attention, we know that when a learner switches his or her attention between two corresponding sources of information trying to learn the content, a split-attention scenario in cognitive processing occurs. Example A is a poor example of instructional strategy that requires the learner to spend extra cognitive resources to switch between two sources of information. The process can impose significant cognitive load irrelevant to the learning. In contrast, Example B eliminates the split-attention scenario by putting the text and diagram on the same page, which not only optimizes the cognitive resources in working memory by eliminating the steps of going back and forth between the text and diagram but also facilitates the mental representation of new information. According to Mayer's cognitive theory of multimedia learning as well as Paivio's dual coding theory,[120,127] presenting text and diagram in proximity enables the learner to effectively formulate the relationship between two sources of information and generate corresponding mental representations.

Developing instructional strategies by taking into account the unique aspects of working memory and its role in human information processing has both theoretical and practical significances. It explicates why some instructional strategies are more effective than others. By grounding the design of instruction in working memory theory, teachers can gain a better understanding of the functional roles and human cognitive processes associated with instructional strategies.

CONCLUSION

This chapter covers the factors related to the working memory performance in terms of the cognitive resources and types of mental load that affect the availability of cognitive resources. The discussions focus primarily on three types of cognitive load—intrinsic, extraneous, and germane cognitive load—and their implications in teaching and learning.

The chapter identifies intrinsic cognitive load as one of the factors that influences working memory performance. Intrinsic cognitive load is defined in terms of the element interactivity in the learning material. A high level of element interactivity suggests the material is difficult to learn and also means the learners will have high intrinsic cognitive load with fewer cognitive resources available. Thus, one of the goals of instructional design is to reduce the intrinsic cognitive load by lowering the element interactivity of the learning material to a level that is challenging but not overwhelming to the learners.

Besides intrinsic cognitive load, the second goal of instructional design related to optimizing working memory performance is to reduce the mental load irrelevant to knowledge construction. This type of cognitive load, known as extraneous cognitive load, is caused by improper design in instruction, which requires learners to perform tasks extraneous to learning.

The third type of cognitive load is related to mental load germane to learning. Mental efforts like solving a problem, making inferences about the trend of economy, and so forth induce mental load on the part of learners. However, this type of mental load is germane to knowledge construction and thus should be increased and maintained to ensure the success of learning.

Based on the discussions we learn that the cognitive resources in working memory are closely related to the level of cognitive load incurred during learning. Intrinsic and extraneous cognitive load can quickly fill the working memory space and make cognitive resources less available for learning, whereas germane cognitive load can still take up a significant portion of working memory space, but it is based on the assumption that cognitive resources are available due to a reduction in extraneous cognitive load. In the next chapter, we will discuss the instructional strategies to reduce intrinsic and extraneous cognitive load and increase germane cognitive load in learning.

FURTHER READING

Chen, O-H., Castro-Alonso, J. C., Paas, F., & Sweller, J. (2018). Extending cognitive load theory to incorporate working memory resource depletion: Evidence from the spacing effect. *Educational Psychology Review*, 30(2), 483–501.

The article uncovers the relations between working memory capacity and cognitive load in learning. The working memory "depletion effect" was examined in conjunction to prolonged mental effort in solving problems that were presented simultaneously compared to problems that were spaced out over the time. Suggestions were made to expand cognitive load theory to incorporate working memory resource depletion in regard to instructional design.

Sweller, J. (2005). Implications of cognitive load theory for multimedia learning. In R. E. Mayer (Ed.), *Cambridge Handbook of Multimedia Learning* (pp. 19–30). New York: Cambridge University Press.

This chapter examines the functions and practices of multimedia learning from a perspective of cognitive load theory. Recommendations are made with regard to the design of multimedia instruction by optimizing the cognitive load during the process of learning.

Sweller, J., Ayres, P., & Kalyuga, S. (2011). *Cognitive Load Theory*. New York: Springer.

The book introduces the cognitive load theory and its theoretical and practical significances in guiding the design of instruction. The focus is on how cognitive load theory can be applied to generating novel and useful instructional procedures to support complex cognitive processes in learning.

Zheng, R., McAlack, M., Wilmes, B., Kohler-Evans, P., & Williamson, J. (2009). Effects of multimedia on cognitive load, self-efficacy, and multiple rule-based problem solving. *British Journal of Educational Technology*, 40(5), 790–803.

This study investigates effects of multimedia on cognitive load, self-efficacy, and learners' ability to solve problems. The findings indicate that providing learners with manipulative function in multimedia facilitates their problem-solving through reduced cognitive load and improved self-efficacy. The study identifies a significant mediator effect for self-efficacy that mediates between multimedia and learners' problem-solving.

Five

Designing Instructional Strategies for Effective Learning

Humans' ability to learn is largely influenced by the working memory functions. The resources in working memory provide the cognitive space critical for active learning such as solving complex problems, discovering new knowledge, and transferring existing knowledge to new learning situations. When cognitive resources are less available, working memory becomes limited in performing the required tasks. As discussed in the proceeding chapter, the availability of cognitive resources is related to several factors, including the learner's schema, the complexity of the content, and the design of the instruction. Instructional strategies that aim to optimize the cognitive resources in working memory have been focused on lowering the element interactivity of complex content, improving the design of instruction, and developing ways to promote cognitive activities related to schema construction.

According to Dinsmore, instructional strategies can be generally categorized into domain-general and domain-specific strategies.[126] Domain-general strategies refer to strategies that can be successfully applied to any domain to support learners' cognitive and metacognitive processes in learning. They include attentional strategies helping individuals focus on important information, organizational strategies aiming at developing learners' abilities like note-taking and outlining, and generative strategies assisting learners in generating new knowledge. Differing from domain-general strategies, domain-specific strategies prescribe strategic processes in an academic domain of interest such as reading, writing, mathematics, and science. The instructional strategies discussed in this chapter fall under the category of domain-general strategies, with a focus on managing the cognitive resources in working memory.

INSTRUCTIONAL STRATEGIES FOR MANAGING COGNITIVE RESOURCES IN WORKING MEMORY

It is important that the instructional strategies aiming at the overall improvement of learner performance attend to the cognitive resources in working memory, making sure that there are sufficient cognitive resources for the learners when they are engaged in knowledge acquisition and schema construction. Cognitive resources refer to the resources within the working memory devoted to cognitive activities during the learning process. Because working memory is limited in its capacity, the cognitive resources within the working memory can also be limited.

Research evidence has shown that individual differences, content difficulty, and design of instruction can influence the availability or the level of cognitive resources in the working memory. Learners with higher working memory capacity are more resourceful in terms of using cognitive resources to handle the complexity of the learning material. In contrast, learners with lower working memory capacity may have difficulty in dealing with complex material because they do not have enough cognitive resources in working memory to encode and decode the information. In addition to individual differences, overly complex materials may exhaust the amount of cognitive resources, making them less available in learning. When the element interactivity of the learning content is high (complex materials), the learner is likely to experience a high cognitive load, which reduces the amount of cognitive resources in working memory accessible for learning. Improper design of instruction is another factor that makes cognitive resources less available for learners. By dealing with content that is improperly designed, the learner will have a hard time learning the content because the improperly designed instruction unnecessarily taxes cognitive resources in working memory.

Evidently, working memory is vulnerable in terms of dealing with content that is either complex or poorly designed. Studies have been conducted to identify instructional strategies that optimize cognitive resources by increasing germane cognitive load in working memory. It is found that instructional strategies that focus on lowering the extraneous cognitive load and increasing the germane cognitive load are beneficial to learners.[128,129] These strategies will be discussed in the later section of this chapter.

The instructional strategies pertinent to intrinsic cognitive load reduction include *pretraining, concept map, worked examples, schema-induced analogy, cognitive prompts*, and *knowledge automaticity*, focusing on schema construction in learning. Similar to intrinsic cognitive load reduction strategies, the strategies aiming at reducing extraneous cognitive load focus on optimizing instructional design to increase cognitive resources in working memory. This line of practice draws from Mayer's cognitive principles of multimedia learning to develop instruction with a focus on *visual and modality presentations*.[120] Different from the previous two types of instructional strategies, which center on reducing intrinsic and extraneous cognitive load, the third type of instructional strategy study finds ways to increase germane cognitive load pertinent to knowledge and schema construction. Instructional strategies in this category include *learner control, self-regulated learning, multiple perspectives,* and *collaboration.* The following sections discuss the types of instructional strategies and their implications for teaching and learning.

Instructional Strategies for Lowering Intrinsic Cognitive Load

As mentioned in Chapter Four, learners' learning can be hampered if the element interactivity involved in the material is too high. High element interactivity can induce high intrinsic cognitive load that causes low performance in learning. However, element interactivity is relative to individual learners. An experienced learner may find the element interactivity of the learning material to be low because he or she may already have the schema in long-term memory. When the information from the new learning material interacts with the schema, a meaningful learning process occurs, causing the new information to be connected with the concepts in the schema, which reduces the element interactivity in new learning. Therefore, learners' schematic knowledge can alleviate the element interactivity as well as intrinsic cognitive load in learning. In this section, the discussion focuses on the instructional strategies that aim to reduce intrinsic cognitive load. They include *pretraining, concept maps, worked examples, schema-induced analogy, cognitive prompts,* and *knowledge automaticity*.

Pretraining

Lacking prior knowledge in the domain can affect learners' abilities to process the material competently. It is often accompanied by high cognitive load and diminishing cognitive resources in working memory. Pretraining is an instructional strategy that focuses on schema construction to lower the element interactivity in learning.

Pollock et al. develop a two-step pretraining approach to improve learners' prior knowledge in learning.[128] The strategy consists of two steps: (a) introducing a simplified version of the complex task and (b) merging the simplified version with the full complex task. In the first step, the provision of an artificial, simplified version of the complex task allows the low prior knowledge learners to learn some of task's fundamental concepts albeit with a limited understanding of the overall process. The temporary ignoring of complex features of the task reduces the low prior knowledge learners' intrinsic cognitive load and, hence, allows them to gain better understanding of the basic concepts of the task. Subsequently, mastery of these basic concepts allows these learners to make sense of the overall task that was previously too complex for them to understand.

The two-step pretraining model proposed by Pollock et al. reduces the element interactivity through schema construction in its initial step. It alleviates the intrinsic cognitive load and affords the learner with more cognitive resources when performing the complex task. By first presenting the basic concepts, the learner experiences a low element interactivity with the content. The initial artificial reduction of element interactivity allows the working memory to have more cognitive resources for processing the basic concepts in the relevant domain. As the learner moves onto more complex content in the second step, the schema built in the first step enables the learner to process the complex task with a reduced cognitive load. Overall, the two-step pretraining model lowers the element interactivity, reduces intrinsic cognitive load, and generates more cognitive resources in working memory for learners to deal with the complex content.

Concept Maps

Like Pollock et al.'s two-step pretraining model, concept maps are effective for building schemas. According to Zheng et al., concept maps are conducive to prior knowledge construction.[129] Concept maps are visual representations of a network of ideas and concepts. They reveal patterns and relationships among the concepts and help students clarify their thinking processes to effectively organize and prioritize information. Figure 5.1 presents an example of concept maps related to photosynthesis in which concept nodes are connected by arrows with the linking verbs indicating the relationships among the concepts.

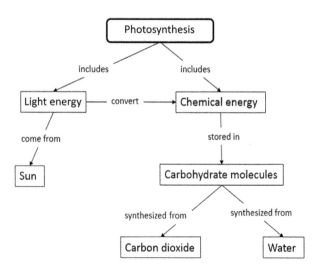

Figure 5.1 An Example of a Concept Map

As a visual tool, the concept maps align with the basic cognitive principles of dual coding theory, which shows that learning becomes more effective and efficient when incoming information is processed through multiple visual formats like text and pictures.[126] Concept maps also mimic the cognitive structures of human thinking. According to Kinchin and Hay, human thinking can be categorized as (a) spoke, (b) hierarchical, and (c) network. These researchers called these categories the cognitive structures of human thinking.[130] Spoke thinking reflects a central to peripheral node relationship in which simple association exists with no understanding of processes or interactions. It is marked by a low level complexity. An example of spoke thinking would be recalling the concept of a table. The learner would think of the concept of table (i.e., the central node) by recalling parts such as the legs and surface of the table (i.e., peripheral nodes). Oftentimes, an addition or loss of a peripheral node (e.g., one table leg) has little effect on the overview. Hierarchical thinking shows a temporal sequence with logic relations between the nodes. It is hierarchical and accumulative. Thus, loss of one link can lose the meaning of the whole hierarchy chain. An example of hierarchical thinking would be learning the principle of a car engine. Missing the knowledge of a carburetor affects the understanding of how a car engine works.

Network thinking has the highest level of complexity. It is marked by a high level of element interactivity where nodes are related in multiple ways. In network thinking, missing one link has little consequence as "other routes" through the network thinking are available and thus can compensate for the missing link. One important feature of network thinking is constant reorganization, a process that refines, organizes, and prioritizes information. The network thinking process reflects a high level element interactivity during which the learner analyzes, synthesizes, and evaluates information through associations and connections (Figure 5.2). Kinchin and Hay find that concept maps simulate types of cognitive structures in thinking and therefore are conducive to schema construction.[130]

Due to space constraints, the focus of our discussion will be on hierarchical concept maps, which are commonly used to help build learners' schemas. The benefits of hierarchical concept maps have been well documented. Puntambekar and Goldstein studied the hierarchical concept maps in science learning and found that learners who learned with concept maps were able to navigate better through the content and engage in better deep learning than those who did not.[131] Roberts and Joiner used the hierarchical concept maps as an educational strategy to help a group of students with autism to learn science.[132] Results indicated that students who studied with concept maps scored better on the achievement test than those who studied without. In a meta-analysis study

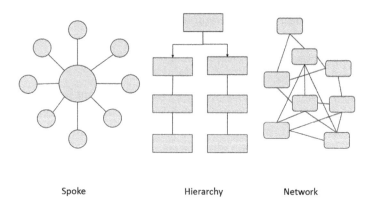

Spoke   Hierarchy   Network

Figure 5.2 Types of Concept Maps

Nesbit and Adesope concluded that studies comparing learning from concept maps to learning from text passages showed that learning with concept maps offered significant learning gains with an average effect size of 0.4.[133] Moreover, significant effect sizes were found for concept maps that facilitated retention and knowledge transfer in learning.

Given the unique visual and cognitive benefits associated with concept maps, Zheng and associates examined the effects of hierarchical concept maps on learners' understanding and knowledge transfer in science.[129] Learners were given the concept maps to learn a science topic with the intention that they would build the schemas to support complex learning. Then follow-up quizzes were given on comprehension and knowledge transfer. Consistent with the findings in previous research, the authors found that the instructional strategy of concept maps had a superior effect on learners' achievement compared to learners without concept maps. They ascribed the success of learners' learning to the unique instructional benefits that the concept maps brought: reduced cognitive load and the development of the schema in the subject area.

Worked Examples

Differing from the instructional strategies discussed previously, worked examples mimic the problem steps to support learners' schemata construction in learning. A worked example is a step-by-step demonstration of how to solve the problem. Usually it involves the initial problem, solution steps, and the final solution to support learners' cognitive skill acquisition.

Research has demonstrated the benefits of worked examples in complex problem-solving. Sweller and Cooper examined the role of worked examples in complex mathematical problem-solving.[134] In their study, the participants viewed half of the examples before they worked on the algebra problems. Results showed that learners who viewed worked examples outperformed those who did not. The authors argued that by studying worked examples, learners were able to develop a schematic understanding of the problem structure, which assisted their problem-solving processes. Booth et al. also concurred that worked examples aided learners' understanding during the problem-solving process.[135] Van Gog, Paas, and van Merrienboer point out that because of its unique role in schematic development, worked examples successfully reduce intrinsic cognitive load during learning.[136] There are two types of worked examples: completion and full worked examples. A completion worked example is a hybrid consisting of a practice assignment and a partial worked example. In completion worked examples, the learner studies the problem with partially provided solution steps, whereas the full worked examples demonstrate all the solution steps. Completion and full worked examples differ in their cognitive functions in terms of supporting learners' learning.

Richey and Nokes-Malach examined how variation in worked examples may impact learners' cognitive performance.[137] They compared completion worked examples with full worked examples in complex learning. Two conditions of worked examples were created: one withheld partial explanation, and the other gave full provision of explanation for the problems. Results revealed that students in the withholding condition demonstrated better conceptual learning and far transfer than did the students in the full provision condition. The authors argued that withholding instructional explanations may provide learners with an opportunity to engage in constructive learning activities to facilitate deeper learning and far transfer, whereas materials that include full explanations could suppress inference generation because the explanatory information is already present, thereby encouraging more passive learning activities such as rehearsal and paraphrasing. However, learners, dependent on their prior knowledge, may respond differently to completion and full worked examples. Completion worked examples may be helpful to experienced learners who are already familiar with the topics of the subject. By working with partial support examples, experienced learners are able to make meaningful connections between the problem state and his or her prior knowledge to develop solutions to the problem. In contrast, novice learners may find completion worked examples less useful as they do not have the adequate schemas to work on the partially supported solutions. Full worked examples would benefit the novice learner because the learner can follow the step-by-step solution to learn how to solve the problem—a process that facilitates the schema construction. In fact, many researchers have called attention to the relationship between instructional strategies and learners' prior knowledge.[138,139] They note that what seems difficult for low prior knowledge learners would be easy for high prior knowledge learners who have already had the knowledge in the pertinent domain. Therefore, full worked examples may create a redundancy effect for experienced learners.

In short, worked examples as an instructional strategy to support learners' schema construction are found to be effective in lowering the element interactivity and therefore reducing intrinsic cognitive load in learning. Two types of worked examples, completion and full worked examples, are commonly used in classrooms to support learners' learning. Prior knowledge may play a key role in determining the effectiveness of worked examples in classrooms. High prior knowledge learners may find completion worked examples to be helpful, whereas low prior knowledge learners may find it detrimental to their learning. In contrast, low prior knowledge learners may find the full worked examples to be beneficial, whereas high prior knowledge learners find them less helpful due to a redundancy effect.

Schema-Induced Analogy

Analogy is an effective cognitive tool for understanding concepts and making meaningful connections between schema and new learning. The construction and effective deployment of analogy require the use of a model to provide systematicity.[140] Several models have been proposed to explicate the analogical reasoning process. Of those models, Sternberg's analogy model is perhaps the most studied and widely applied.[141] According to Sternberg, analogical reasoning essentially consists of encoding, inference, mapping, application, and response. The process promotes the interaction between the content and the learner's schema. Holyoak and Thagard noted that analogies are related to a large network of knowledge structure (i.e., schema) and that they can be primed to new learning.[142]

Analogy, especially schema-induced analogy, requires the learner to understand the analogy through an activation of prior knowledge. For example, when teaching a new subject like atoms, the complex new subject may take root in the learner's mind through an activation of prior knowledge by telling him or her that the atom resembles a miniature solar system. That is, the structure (sun and planets) and the relationship (gravitational and counter-gravitational forces) of the solar system are cognitively transferred to a new subject like atoms in which the structure (atom and its particles, namely, protons, neutrons, and electrons) and the relationship (positive and negative charges) are similar to the structure and relationship of the solar system.

The way that an analogy works is by mapping the base concept to the target concept as in the example of an analogy between solar system and atom structure. The study of the solar system activates the learner's prior knowledge about the solar system. The activated prior knowledge is then mapped onto the structure of an atom, completing the process of transferring knowledge from the base concept to the target concept. Zheng, Yang, Garcia, and McCadden studied the effects of schema-induced analogical reasoning on learners' abilities to learn the electric circuit (Figure 5.3).[143] The learners' schemas were activated through a multimedia presentation during which they studied a water system and its related

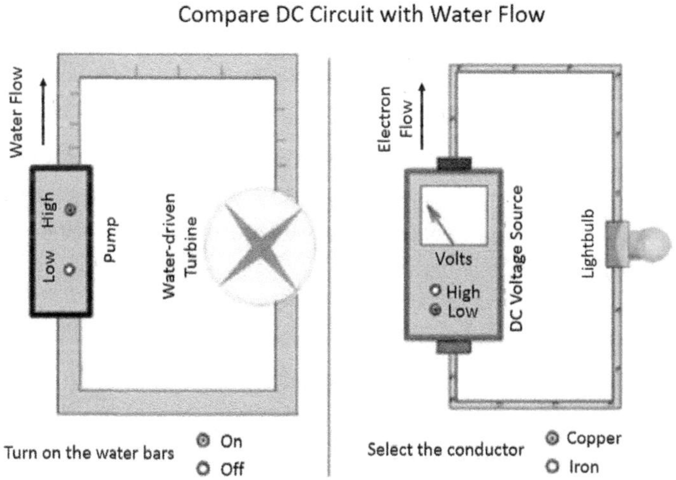

Compare DC Circuit with Water Flow

Figure 5.3 An Example of Schema-Induced Analogical Reasoning

concepts: water pump, water pipes, and water turbine. They further studied the relationship between water speed and power by turning the bars in the water pipe vertically on and off. The learners learned that when the bars were turned vertically on, the resistance to the water flowing from the pump to the turbine increased, thus a higher pressure from the water pump was needed to maintain an appropriate water speed to keep the turbine running. The water pump system activated learners' schemas about the relationships among resistance, power, and current, which were later mapped onto the electric circuit system where the battery is analogical to the water pump, the water current is similar to electric current, and the bars in the water pipe resemble the resistance in the electrical current. Zheng et al.'s study reveals that schema-induced analogical reasoning helps the learners better understand the concepts in new content through an activation of prior knowledge in something they are familiar with. It also shows that the schema-induced analogy (a) facilitates the transition from concrete learning to abstract learning and (b) makes cognitive resources available in working memory through the reduction of cognitive load.

In sum, schema-induced analogical reasoning has been used as an instructional strategy to lower element interactivity and alleviate the intrinsic cognitive load in complex learning through schema activation.

Cognitive Prompts

Cognitive prompts have been widely used in a variety of situations to support learners' deep and critical thinking.[144] Like the instructional strategies previously discussed, cognitive prompts focus on the activation of and connection with the schemas to support meaningful and deep learning. Learners become engaged in self-reflection and thinking deeply about the problems with cognitive prompts.

Cognitive prompts are learning questions placed throughout an educational presentation that help scaffold learners' thinking processes. There are different types of cognitive prompts focusing on learners' abilities to elaborate ideas, organize information, make predictions, engage in reflective thinking, and make inferences. Table 5.1 lists the prompt types and questions relevant to particular subject areas.

Table 5.1 Examples of Cognitive Prompts and Questions

Subject Area	Prompt Type	Prompt Examples
Science	Elaborating ideas, views, and concepts	"Which examples can you think of that illuminate, confirm, or conflict with the climate change hypothesis?"
Language Arts	Stimulating organization	"Judging from your past experiences, how do you best organize an essay?"
Reading	Making prediction	"The baby bear just woke up and is hungry. What do you think he will do now?"
Mathematics	Think reflectively	"What would you do differently to find the supplementary angle in Problem 1.2 in Exercise 4?"
Science	Making inferences	"Noting the bird has a pair of large eye sockets, what kind of bird do you think it is, the one that is active at night or during the day?"

Cognitive prompts are widely used for promoting deep learning by making meaningful connections with learners' schemas. For example, the cognitive prompt of "Judging from your past experiences, how do you best organize an essay?" prompts the learner to think about ways to organize an essay based on his or her past experience. Zheng and associates studied the role of cognitive prompts in learners' schema activation in caregiving training.[145,146] The learners received video training on the related topics. Cognitive prompts were embedded in the videos to activate learners' schemas when studying complex, specialized topics like dementia. By prompting the learners to relate to their personal experiences or prior knowledge about the subject, the learners were able to understand the complex relationship between behavioral and emotional symptoms associated with dementia caregiving. The results showed a superior effect for cognitive prompts as measured by comprehension and knowledge transfer. Zheng and associates concluded that schema activation through cognitive prompts enabled learners to meaningfully connect their prior knowledge with the new learning content.

The amount of prior knowledge that learners have is an important determinant of the effectiveness of cognitive prompt strategy. The more information a learner already has about a topic, the greater the benefits from cognitive prompts.

Knowledge Automaticity

Research suggests that there is little one can do to alter the complexity and difficulty of the content. However, the situation can be changed with an increase of one's schema in the subject area. Instructional strategies like pretraining, worked examples, concept mapping, and so on are attempts to build schemas to circumvent the intrinsic cognitive load, that is, by building schemas (i.e., an increase in prior knowledge), the learner is able to process the content with reduced element interactivity. Knowledge automaticity is another way of bypassing the intrinsic cognitive load in learning.

In Chapter Two we discussed the rehearsal process in working memory. The longer material is kept alive in short-term memory, the greater the likelihood that it would be transferred to long-term memory. Knowledge automaticity is the process of repeating the materials again and again until they become part of our schemas. Some argue that rehearsal does not land in transferring information into long-term memory because repeating information in the rehearsal process does not involve thinking about its meaning or connecting it to other information.[147] However, van Merrienboer proposes that with adequate cognitive support, a rehearsal strategy can lead to knowledge automaticity with information meaningfully encoded in long-term memory.[148]

Cognitive scientists believe that automatized information retrieved from long-term memory can be processed in chunks and often at an unconscious level. Take an example in reading. A sophisticated reader does not consciously decipher the meaning of each word when reading a Harry Potter novel. Rather, the words are automatically processed at the contextual, as opposed to semantic, level to generate the meaning for the learner.

Content difficulty can be a challenge to learners. Difficult material means high element interactivity, hence high intrinsic cognitive load during learning. Knowledge automaticity through rehearsal can alleviate the intrinsic cognitive load that results in greater cognitive resources being available for learning.

Instructional Strategies for Reducing Extraneous Cognitive Load

Extraneous cognitive load is detrimental to learning because it imposes irrelevant cognitive load on the learner during learning. High extraneous cognitive load means few cognitive resources available in working memory. Efforts have been made to reduce extraneous cognitive load with instructional strategies focusing on (a) minimizing the irrelevant cognitive load in learning and (b) increasing the cognitive resources in working memory through optimal design in instruction. The following section discusses instructional strategies aiming to reduce extraneous cognitive load.

Visual-Visual Strategy

Learners' spatial abilities play an important role in learning that requires spatial processing of the information. Topics related to spatial processing include geography, biology, chemistry, mathematics, physics, and so forth. Spatial ability is defined as one's ability to perform spatially related tasks like spatial perception, mental rotation, and spatial visualization. For example, reading a map is associated with an individual's ability to perceive the spatial relationship between the objects (spatial perception), whereas playing a Rubik's cube is related to one's ability to mentally rotate the sides to find the solution (mental rotation), and describing what a building looks like based on an architectural blueprint demonstrates one's ability to visualize the object in three-dimensional form (spatial visualization).

In situations where visuals like diagrams aid the performance on spatially related tasks, adding the visuals to the text optimizes learners' performance in terms of mental representation formation, deeper understanding, and reduction of cognitive load.[127,149] Paivio describes visual processing in working memory by showing that presenting information with both text and image (visual-visual) facilitates learners' mental representation in working memory.[127] Figure 5.4 compares the role of visual-visual strategy with visual only strategy in spatial ability-related geometry learning. Example A shows a visual-only presentation strategy in which the learner solves the geometry problem without the visual diagram. In solving the geometry problem, the learner has to memorize the information while also mentally visualizing the triangle, the angles, and the values of angles. The mental visualization process induces extraneous cognitive load that is superfluous to geometry learning. Example B presents the visual-visual strategy in which both diagram and text are included in geometry problem-solving. As the learner goes through the text, he or she can easily reference the diagram for the information in

The triangle ABC is a regular triangle. Angle ABC is 30°; angle BCA is 65°. Find the value of angle BAC.

The triangle ABC is a regular triangle. Angle ABC is 30°; angle BCA is 65°. Find the value of angle BAC.

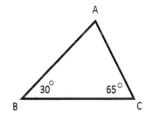

Example A   Example B

Figure 5.4 Visual-Only versus Visual-Visual Instructional Strategy

the text. That is, instead of spending cognitive resources to mentally figure out what and where the angles are, the learner can devote the same cognitive resources to problem-solving.

This discussion demonstrates the advantages of the visual-visual instructional strategy, which facilitates learners' mental representation. However, although the visual-visual strategy reduces extraneous cognitive load by eliminating the mental visualization process compared to the text-only strategy, presenting information through both visual sources (text and diagram) can potentially hinder learners' learning. We will visit this issue in the next section.

Visual-Audio Strategy

Mayer and colleagues studied the effects of modality in multimedia learning and found that the difficulty in processing information through one sensory channel (e.g., visual) could be alleviated by delivering the information through multiple sensory channels (e.g., visuals and audios).[120,121] It is possible that learners may become visually overwhelmed with the visual-visual strategy because coordinating different sources of visual information in one channel may add cognitive load to the information processing regardless of its cognitive benefit in mental representation formation. In light of visual-visual dilemma, Clark et al. wrote, "One way to reduce load imposed by the need to coordinate visuals and words is to divide the new incoming content among the two storage areas in working memory—the visual and auditory" (p. 61).[149]

Empirical evidence in research has shown that adding narration to visuals supports learners' comprehension and knowledge transfer. Ioannou, Rodiou, and Iliou studied the effects of narration and visuals on learners' abilities in learning triangles.[150] Two study conditions were created: (a) pictures with narration and (b) pictures with on-screen text. In the pictures with narration condition, learners viewed and listened to a presentation of triangles, whereas in the pictures with on-screen text condition, the learners viewed the pictures with on-screen text. A recall test was administered after the learning period. Results indicated that students in the pictures with narration condition demonstrated better comprehension than did those in the pictures with on-screen text condition. The authors concluded that learners were more likely to build connections among corresponding words and pictures when words were presented in a spoken form (narration) simultaneously with pictures. An early study by Tindall-Ford, Chandler, and Sweller showed similar results.[151] The researchers examined the differences between visual-audio and visual-visual strategies. Two study conditions were created: (a) a diagram about an electrical test with the text explaining the electrical testing process and (b) a diagram with audio narration using the same words presented in the first condition. Dependent on the condition, the learners learned the content either in visual-visual or visual-audio format, followed by a written problem-solving quiz and a practical test that required the learners to perform the electrical test using actual equipment. It was found that the learners in the diagram with audio narration condition outperformed the ones in the diagram with text condition in both measures.

Overall, research has demonstrated a superior effect of visual-audio strategy in learning. Studies have shown that the visual-visual strategy is superior over the visual-only strategy and that the visual-audio strategy is more effective than the visual-visual strategy in terms of cognitive load reduction, performance, and achievement.

Keywords-Audio Strategy

In Chapter Four we mentioned the instructional strategy of on-screen text, graphic, and narration can hinder learners' learning (Figure 4.1). According to Mayer and Johnson, the process of mentally organizing the verbal and pictorial representations into coherent cognitive structures in working memory can be interrupted when the narration is added to the presentation.[152] The addition of narration forces two visuals (verbal and pictorial representations) to compete with each other as the learner has to visually scan between the text and the graphic to mentally reconcile the incoming spoken and verbal stream. That is, the on-screen text creates a redundancy effect by wasting the learner's limited cognitive resources on extraneous processing. As a result, the learner is less able to engage in the cognitive processing needed for learning.

Research suggests that attention plays a key role in essential and generative processes in learning (also see discussions on attention in Chapter Two). Mayer and Johnson developed the *keywords and audio* strategy by hypothesizing that animation, narration, and keywords (not the text verbatim of the narration) would minimize the redundancy effect and improve learners' learning by directing their attention to key information in the learning material.[150] In their study, the keywords were placed next to the diagram to direct learners' visual attention to the key portion of the diagram. Instead of creating a redundancy effect, the design of animation and narration with keywords proved to be effective for learners' learning. It was found that the keywords directed the learners' attention to the essential information and thereby reduced the extraneous cognitive load. The results confirmed the researchers' hypothesis, showing a superior effect for keywords and audio strategy as measured by comprehension and transfer in learning.

Teachers may find the keywords-audio strategy useful in that it (a) eliminates wasteful processing of entire sentences with two or three keywords instead of entire sentences, (b) saves the learner's effort of scanning from the bottom of the screen to points in the diagram by placing the keywords next to the corresponding elements in the diagram, and (c) enhances the instructional function of narration with keywords directing learners' attention to important information.

Visual Proximity Strategy

Corresponding instructional sources like graphic and text, when placed separately, can cause split attention in learning (see Figure 4.2). With instructional material that places the information sources far from each other, learners will have to split their attention to visually search the page or screen for corresponding words and pictures. The result is that it creates split attention in learning. Split attention induces extraneous cognitive load due to the extra mental effort required of the learner to coordinate among different sources of information. To mitigate the split-attention effect, Mayer proposes that corresponding information sources (e.g., words and pictures) must be placed close to each other on the page or screen so that the learner is able to hold them both in working memory at the same time. Mayer defines it as *spatial contiguity principle* in multimedia learning.[120]

The spatial contiguity principle has been widely tested. Mayer and colleagues examined the difference between instructional sources that were spatially proximate to each other and the ones that were far from each other.[153,154] Their studies yielded consistent results showing learners who received printed text and pictures near each other (integrated presentation group) generated more solutions to the problem-solving transfer questions than did learners who received printed text and pictures far from each other (separated presentation group). The authors argued that placing corresponding words and pictures in spatial contiguity (i.e., close to each other) resulted in better performance on knowledge transfer because learners did not need to spend extra cognitive resources searching through information in the text and picture that were spatially far from each other. Consequently, learners were less likely to suffer from a working memory overload induced by extraneous cognitive load.

The visual proximity strategy provides a tool for teachers to develop multimedia-based instructional materials in classrooms. By understanding the role of cognitive load associated with the visual processing in learning, teachers will be able to design effective multimedia, especially visual materials, to support learners' learning.

Visual-Audio Temporal Strategy

Whereas the spatial contiguity principle focuses on the spatial aspects of presentation, the principle of temporal contiguity in multimedia learning emphasizes the contiguity of presenting instructional materials in time. Presenting animated material simultaneously with narration, for example, is an example of the temporal contiguity principle. A violation of the principle by separating the animated material from the narration (noncontiguity) would disrupt the building of referential connections between the animation and narration. Mayer points out that when corresponding information sources (e.g., animation and narration) are presented at the *same time* (note: as opposed to in the *same place* in spatial contiguity), the learner is able to hold both information sources in working memory and build the mental representation through referential connections.[120]

Mayer and colleagues tested the temporal contiguity principle by presenting corresponding animation and narration (a) simultaneously and (b) successively. In eight tests, the results showed that students who received corresponding segments of animation and narration simultaneously performed better on generating solutions to problems than did students who received the same segments successively.[155,156] Mayer et al. explained that the simultaneous presentation of animation and narration aligned well with the cognitive theory of human architecture of the brain.[156] The information from different sensory sources gets processed simultaneously in the visual and auditory channels, which are cross-referenced to form mental representations in learning.

In contrast, the successive approach in which the animation and narration are presented successively hinders learning. The severance of animation and narration imposes an extraneous cognitive load on working memory. That is, only a small part of information from narration remains in the verbal working memory when the animation begins. In Chapter Two we discussed that the information held in auditory sensory memory stays for only a relatively short amount of time and that information in visual sensory memory can be overwritten by new information. The narrative information held in working memory can fade quickly when the learner starts processing the information in animation. It is evident that the successive approach puts learners' ability to build mental representations in jeopardy due to the information fading and the disruption between narrative and visual information sources.

This research supports the visual-audio temporal strategy in instructional design. As teachers apply multimedia to their classroom teaching, the visual-audio temporal strategy will help them identify optimal design in integrating animation and narration to their teaching.

Further Considerations about Visual Proximity and Visual-Audio Temporal Strategies

The discussion on visual proximity and visual-audio temporal strategies demonstrates that both strategies support the building of learners' mental representations, reduce their extraneous cognitive load by minimizing the split-attention effect, and make cognitive resources available in working memory. Both strategies are based on the same underlying assumption— learners are better able to build connections between two sources of information when they can mentally process them at the same time.

In spite of the similarities, there are some distinctions between the two strategies. First, visual proximity strategy is based on spatial contiguity principle in multimedia learning and thus focuses on the spatial aspect of information sources. Its design approach is to place corresponding visuals close to each other to support referential connections and mental representations, whereas visual-audio temporal strategy, which is built on temporal contiguity principle in multimedia learning, accentuates the importance of presenting visual and auditory materials at the same time. The synchronization of visual and auditory information enables working memory to simultaneously process both types of information in their respective channels for referential connections and mental representations. Second, from a sensory perspective, the visual proximity strategy involves developing instructional materials processed by eyes. That is, only the visual channel is involved. Therefore, teachers should be strategic when using the visual proximity strategy because too much visual information can overwhelm the visual channel, causing a cognitive overload. On the other hand, visual-audio temporal strategy involves both ears and eyes (e.g., narration and animation). That is, the incoming information is processed separately by the visual and auditory channels, which are cross-referenced and coordinated to support mental representations without cognitive overload. Understanding these differences can help teachers better design their instructional materials for learning.

Cueing and Signaling

Cueing and signaling are effective instructional strategies to draw learners' attention to critical portions of complex visual materials (see Chapter Two for the discussion of cueing). Learners become disoriented when learning a complex topic like the cardiovascular system. Visual cues (e.g., arrows and lines) can help learners identify essential information and direct their attention to key portions of the content. Clark et al. point out that cueing and signaling can speed learners' information processing in visually related learning by redirecting their attention to key information in the complex content and reducing extraneous cognitive load by avoiding having to search through irrelevant information.[149]

Studies on cueing and signaling have yielded interesting findings. de Koning and colleagues examined the effects of animation on learning.[157] Learners were randomly assigned to cueing and noncueing conditions to study the cardiovascular system. Results revealed that cueing not only enhanced learners' comprehension and knowledge transfer but also reduced the extraneous cognitive load. An early study by Tabbers and colleagues showed similar outcomes.[158] They found visual cues increased the effectiveness of multimedia instructions in terms of better learning outcomes with less mental effort.

However, Richter, Scheiter, and Eitel caution that the study of signaling should be placed within the framework of individual differences in terms of prior knowledge.[159] In their study they found mixed outcomes about the signaling strategy in regard to learners' prior knowledge. It was found that lower prior knowledge learners benefited from the signaling, whereas high prior knowledge learners were hindered by the same strategy.

The instructional strategies of cueing and signaling are widely used in education. Understanding their cognitive functionality in learning would help teachers better apply the strategies in teaching in terms of supporting learners' cognitive information processing, reducing extraneous cognitive load, and facilitating mental representations in learning.

Instructional Strategies for Optimizing Germane Cognitive Load

Working memory performance is partially determined by the amount of cognitive resources available during learning. Cognitive load can affect the availability of cognitive resources in working memory. As discussed earlier, intrinsic and extraneous cognitive load are detrimental to learning by overloading the working memory either with high element interactivity or improper design in instruction. Therefore, they must be reduced during the learning process.[160]

The three types of cognitive load (i.e., intrinsic, extraneous, and germane cognitive load) form the total cognitive load in working memory. The three cognitive loads are additive. From an instructional design perspective, the design of instruction should decrease extraneous cognitive load and increase germane load, which is related to knowledge and schema construction. This is, however, based on the premise that the total cognitive load stays within the limits of working memory. So far, our discussion has been on instructional strategies to lower the intrinsic and extraneous cognitive load to make cognitive resources available in learning.

However, the availability of cognitive resources does not guarantee meaningful learning. That is, learning does not necessarily happen even with cognitive resources available due to a reduction of element interactivity or an elimination of improper design in instruction. Instructional strategies must be developed to effectively utilize the available cognitive resources to engage learners in meaningful constructive and innovative learning. Two important aspects are associated with this learning process. One is the learner's ability to construct schemas, and the other is the effort to engage in constructing schemas. In the following sections, we discuss instructional strategies aiming at developing learners' abilities to construct schemas and increase their germane cognitive load in learning. Strategies increasing germane cognitive load include *learner control, self-regulated learning, multiple perspectives,* and *collaborative learning.*

Learner Control

Motivation is considered to be a necessary antecedent for learning.[161] One of the strategies in motivational learning is giving students control in their learning. The learner control principle posits that giving learners control over their instruction by allowing them to pace, sequence, and select information aids learning. The cognitive and metacognitive benefits associated with learner control approach include: (a) affording an active, constructive processing of learning materials,

(b) increasing and sustaining the motivation to learn, and (c) enabling learners to adapt instruction to their preferences and needs.

Research evidence has demonstrated the relationship between motivation and learning. Um, Plass, Homer, and Hayward investigated the emotions (positive vs. neutral emotions) related to learner performance.[125] The researchers found that positive emotions increased the amount of learners' reported mental effort, which was further positively correlated with the learning outcome. In a three-way study on worked examples, expertise, and content difficulty in mathematics, Gupita reported, among other findings, a significant correlation between interest and germane cognitive load. These findings suggest that motivation is correlated with and induces germane cognitive load.[162]

Studies show that learner control significantly influences learners' performance, motivation, and germane cognitive load. In their study on the relations between academic emotions, control belief, learning disorientation, and cognitive load, Sunawan and Xiong found control belief as a mediator between emotion and cognitive load.[163] Their findings further revealed control belief as an antecedent for positive emotion, which in turn evoked germane cognitive load in learning. Chang Liang, Chou, and Lin examined game-based versus non-game-based learning and discovered that the learners' mental load (germane to learning) and motivation increased when learning with serious games in which they had the control of the learning process.[164]

As an instructional strategy, learner control has been used to support learners' learning in terms of increasing germane cognitive load, that is, mental effort toward schema construction and providing motivation in learning. Approaches related to learner control like self-study, adaptive learning, learner choice, and learner-centered discovery learning have been used in classrooms to improve students' motivation and vested interest in learning.

Self-Regulated Learning

Similar to learner control, self-regulated learning refers to a process of taking control of and evaluating one's own learning behavior, particularly developing learners' metacognitive thinking (e.g., thinking about one's learning or learning strategies), strategic action (e.g., planning, monitoring, and evaluating personal progress), and motivation to learn.[165] Research evidence shows that strategies like task analysis, goal setting, self-explanation, and self-evaluation facilitate learners' metacognitive thinking in terms of thinking about their learning, planning, and monitoring learning progress.[166,167] MacArthur, Philippakos, and Ianetta employed self-regulated strategy instruction to teach writing to college students.[168] Multiple self-regulation strategies were provided to support student learning, which included self-monitoring, self-evaluation, self-instructions, goal setting, self-reinforcement, and management of time and environment along with constructive feedback to develop students' abilities in generating and organizing content. Significant positive effects were found for overall quality of writing as well as self-efficacy and mastery motivation.

There has been consistent evidence showing the relationship between germane cognitive load and self-regulation in learning.[169,170] It is believed that self-regulation is supported by multiple variables including motivation and mental effort to achieve the learning goals. When learning is self-regulated, coupled with the efforts of self-monitoring and self-planning, the mental effort associated with such learning is initiated. Cook et al. noticed a positive correlation between germane cognitive load, motivation, and self-regulation.[169]

However, researchers caution that the germane cognitive load induced by self-regulated learning and motivation should not exceed the overall limit of working memory.[160] When the effort to construct knowledge becomes overly taxing on the working memory, unintended consequences may occur, such as diminishing motivation and frustration in learning. In such a situation the cognitive load, which was germane to learning, turns into something that hinders learning.[171] Therefore, as teachers implement self-regulated learning strategy in their teaching to optimize learners' germane cognitive load for knowledge construction, it is important to manage the germane cognitive load properly by keeping it within the overall working memory limit.

Multiple Perspectives

Multiple perspectives in learning have been an effective instructional strategy to elicit the germane cognitive load in learning. Broadly defined, the term *multiple perspectives* refers to the practice of encompassing multiple and possibly heterogeneous viewpoints, representations, and roles that can be adopted within both a collaborative and non-collaborative context. Multiple perspectives strategy in education has been adopted by teachers to teach students to think and examine issues through diverse aspects and multiple lenses.

The strategy of multiple perspectives enables learners to examine the issues through different perspectives, which in turn deepens their understanding about the issues and improves their abilities to think critically.[172] It also motivates learners to learn because multiple perspectives provide learners the opportunity to explore and find solutions in different contexts. Considering the example of learning the Pythagorean Theorem in mathematics (Figure 5.5). Instead of employing the traditional didactic approach to teaching the Pythagorean Theorem, the multiple perspective learning strategy encourages learners to explore the issue and solve the problem with the Pythagorean Theorem in different contexts: building a truss, finding the hypotenuse of an eighteenth-century crane, and determining the length of the main cable of the suspense bridge. It is evident that when learning is situated in rich, multiple contexts like Figure 5.5, learners will show more interest toward the subject.

This example supports the notion that as an instructional strategy, multiple perspectives help students understand deeply about the content. The multiple perspectives in Figure 5.5 help learners become aware that there is more than one way to solve the hypotenuse problem. For example, the length of hypotenuse can be obtained through 45-, 45-, and 90-degree triangles or 30-, 60-, and 90-degree triangles using Pythagorean Theorem. Moreover, the multiple perspective strategy bridges the connection between the abstract concept (e.g., the Pythagorean Theorem) and the real world

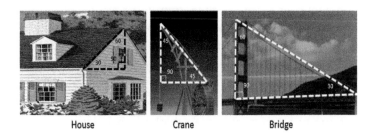

House   Crane   Bridge

Figure 5.5 Multiple Perspectives in Problem-Solving

by presenting the topic in different contexts: the trusses of a house, the arm of a crane, and the main cable of a suspense bridge.

In sum, multiple perspective strategy enables learners to think deeply by studying the content through diverse lenses. It offers the opportunity to engage in dialogues at both internal and external levels through self-reflection and interaction with the contexts. As such, it has become a useful tool by teachers to promote cognitive (e.g., cognitive flexibility) and affective (e.g., motivation or interest) aspects in learning as well as learners' sustained germane cognitive load in knowledge and schema construction.

Collaborative Learning

Collaborative learning is widely believed to be an effective teaching approach; it can enhance learners' social interaction and offer a learning environment that provides rich learning experiences. Collaborative learning refers to the process of people or groups of people working together to accomplish a learning goal. Teams that work collaboratively often access greater resources and thus increase the chance of success as they engage in collaborative problem-solving or learning.

Collaborative learning involves individuals and the environment over space and time, signaling a process of socially distributed cognition in learning.[173] Within a collaborative learning environment, the cognitive processing associated with learning is off-loaded into the group; that is, the cognition is processed collectively by the members of the group. Vasciliou and associates studied collaboration and social structures of two groups of learners working on a design problem and observed the impact of collective cognitive processing on learners' achievement in collaborative learning.[174]

In addition to the cognitive benefits, research evidence has also shown the benefits related to affective aspects in learning. Chen, Wang, and Lin investigated the collaborative modes of game-based learning in promoting learners' science learning and motivation.[175] Learners were randomly assigned to a solitary condition or a collaborative group condition. Results revealed a superior effect for the collaborative group condition compared to the solitary condition as measured by performance and motivation outcomes. Retnowati, Ayres, and Sweller compared collaborative learning with individual learning in sixth graders' mathematics.[176] Learners were more motivated in collaborative learning when engaged in problem-solving than did those in individual learning.

Collaborative learning, known for its collective process and socially distributed cognition among the team members, is deemed to be effective in motivating students to learn because working collectively tends to develop in learners a sense of community and involvement. However, the benefits of collaborative learning appear only in positive and well-functioning teams. Merely dividing learners into learning groups cannot guarantee effective collaborative learning to occur.[177, 178] When developing collaborative learning, it is important to put the following key factors in perspective. They include (a) identifying group goal(s), (b) building trust among group members, (c) promoting group interaction, (d) including authentic experience, (e) scaffolding collaborative learning activities, (f) incorporating technology, and (g) embracing diversity. Table 5.2 presents the key factors critical to effective collaborative learning with discussions on the roles of the factors.

It is important to understand these factors and their roles when developing collaborative learning. Collaboration is a learned process. By incorporating the factors shown in

Table 5.2 Key Factors for Effective Collective Learning

Key Factors	Discussions
Identify group goal(s)	It is important to establish an unambiguous group goal, that is, what the group intends to accomplish. This keeps the group on task as the members engaged in learning activities.
Build trust among group members	Developing cooperative and trustful relationships among the members is key to the success of collaborative learning. Strategies like open communication help build trust and facilitate healthy member relationships.
Promote group interaction	Collaborative learning is based on the interaction among group members. Thus, creating an environment promoting member interaction is essential in making collaborative learning a successful experience for learners.
Include authentic experience	For collaborative learning to be meaningful, the learning content should include real-world problems. Studies show that real-world problems make learning experiences authentic and fit well with the scope for collaborative learning.
Scaffold collaborative learning activities	Collaborative learning, especially problem-based learning, can be challenging to novice learners. Scaffolding provides necessary cognitive and metacognitive support to learners' deeper-level thinking and abilities to analyze, synthesize, and evaluate information and create new knowledge.
Incorporate technology	Research shows that modern technologies like social blogging, online discussion forums, online chat-room, webinars, and so on make collaborative learning easier. Evidence indicates that more exchanges related to planning, rather than challenging viewpoints, occurred more frequently through online interactions. It is also known that technology may change the flow of information and refine the social cognitive structure in learning.

Key Factors	Discussions
Embrace diversity	In collaborative learning, learners impart ideas and share perspectives with others. An environment that embraces diversity in values, beliefs, and cultures and teaches the value of multiplicity in thought enriches the process of collaborative learning, making it productive and constructive. Class discussions emphasizing the need for different perspectives and encouraging independent thinking, for example, enable learners to understand the issues at a deeper level, which improves their abilities to solve complex problems.

Table 5.2, teachers are able to develop an effective collaborative learning environment that nurtures learners' multiple perspectives, promotes their independent thinking, and enhances their critical and analytical skills. Collaborative learning, if managed correctly, can be a powerful tool that allows learners to tap into new ideas and information that become innovative and creative in learning.

OPTIMIZING COGNITIVE INFORMATION PROCESSING WITH EMERGING LEARNING TECHNOLOGY

The advancement in digital technology offers tremendous opportunities for teaching and learning. Emerging new technologies like AI, augmented and virtual realities, and learning analytics have shown promises in education by transforming the paradigms in learners' cognitive thinking and learning. A brief discussion of these technologies and their implications in cognitive information processing and the design of instruction are provided in the following section.

AI and Individualized Learning

AI technology has increasingly found its presence in education to support students' cognitive learning. The term *artificial intelligence* (AI) describes the processing of information by machines in contrast to the natural intelligence displayed by humans and other animals. Thus, AI is sometimes called machine intelligence. There are three types of AIs: (a) analytical AI, (b) human-inspired AI, and (c) humanized AI.

Analytical AI

Analytical AI simulates human cognitive intelligence by generating cognitive representations of the world. It builds its algorithms based on human schemas to guide the learning process. Examples of analytical AI include intelligent tutoring and AI-based learning systems.

Human-Inspired AI

Differing from analytical AI, which focuses on cognitive aspects, human-inspired AI attends to both cognitive and emotional performances. By collecting and synthesizing the data sources (e.g., cognitive and emotional), human-inspired AI is able to discern learners' cognitive paths and emotional status to make recommendations pertaining to learners' learning and the content to be delivered.

Humanized AI

Humanized AI is similar to human-inspired AI in that it is capable of performing cognitive and emotional tasks. At the same time, humanized AI is different from human-inspired AI because it shows characteristics of all types of competences, that is, cognitive, emotional, and social intelligence, along with being capable of natural language processing. It is self-conscious and self-aware in its interactions with others. Learners can directly communicate with humanized AI devices through natural language. Examples of humanized AI include service robots, AI butlers, AI home controllers, Apple Siri, and Amazon Alexa.

Analytical AI and Its Implications in Learning

Although AI technology has overall shown great potential in learners' cognitive learning, analytical AI has seen its future inroads into the classrooms. Figure 5.6 shows an example of AI-based automatic visual cueing for reading. The analytical AI system, which is still in its conceptual stage, consists of a noninvasive eye-track device that is integrated with analytical AI. The eye tracker collects data from the learner's eye movements and pupil dilation. The data are then fed into the analytical AI system to determine (a) how well the learner understands the content, (b) which knowledge components are missing in the learner's schema, and (c) which information is critical to the individual learner's knowledge structure. The AI system then responds to the learner's performance by providing visual cues directing him or her to key information in the reading paragraph.

The cognitive benefits of the AI learning system include (a) providing learners' on-the-spot cognitive support through instant cognitive diagnosis and (b) alleviating extraneous cognitive load with visual cues by directing the learner's attention to key portions of the learning material. Traditional eye-tracking research follows a two-step protocol by first collecting the eye-tracking data and then modifying the intervention for further improvement based on the eye-tracking data. The problem with the traditional approach in eye-tracking research is that if a reader cannot process the reading material correctly, say by failing to identify the key factors

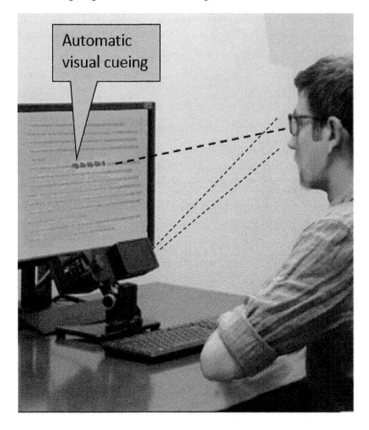

Figure 5.6 AI-based Automatic Visual Cueing

(e.g., sun, water, or carbon dioxide) in photosynthesis, then the eye tracker can do little to help the reader on the spot. This is because traditional eye-tracking research takes a posteriori approach in intervention. In contrast, the AI system in Figure 5.6 can customize the individual learner's learning by identifying the problems based on real-time data and providing instant instructional support to the learner.

In addition to visual cueing, the analytical AI technology can be used to support other instructional strategies like cognitive prompts, worked examples, and concept mapping to enhance students' schema construction in learning.

Augmented and Virtual Realities

Augmented reality (AR) and virtual reality (VR) are becoming increasingly common forms of technologies in education. VR is generally associated with devices that provide immersive, virtual experience of corresponding real-world environments. There are considerable benefits for VR application in educational settings. The early aviation pilot training simulator is an example of a VR technology application in education. Recent applications of VR in education have aimed to develop learners' critical thinking in science learning,[179] teach complex learning content, [180] and provide motivational support for engaged learning.[181]

The cognitive and educational benefits associated with VR learning are palpable: It can take students on a field trip without leaving the classroom; break down global geographic and social barriers in which students can experience cultures all over the world; explain complex concepts and ideas, which were otherwise impossible in traditional settings, to young minds; and experience the impossible by reenacting the life of the Bronze Age, for example. The motivation elicited by the VR learning experience can be transferred to a sustained mental effort that reflects the germane cognitive load in learning.

Different from VR, AR represents the effort to augment the existing content with computer-generated interactive experiences through sensory inputs like audio, visuals, and haptic manipulations. Poitras and associates explored the role of AR technology in supporting learners' learning in a history museum.[182] They found that the AR technology that integrates with a variety of media (e.g., videos, images, and audio) and devices (e.g., tablets and smartphones) significantly improved learners' understanding of the content as well as their interest in the subject.

Figure 5.7 presents an example of AR application in a classroom where students are learning about an endangered species of bird. The textbook on the table contains a picture of the endangered bird. To help students gain a better understanding about the living habitat, the food chain, and the climate related to the endangered bird, the teacher employs AR to support her students' learning. Students use the tablet that is AR capable and scan the picture in the textbook. Immediately, an interactive video appears on the tablet describing the living habitat of the endangered bird. Students are able to

Figure 5.7 An Example of AR

interact with the content by touching on the spots (e.g., lake, trees, etc.) in the video to search for information.

In short, VR creates a learning experience by immersing learners in a computer-generated environment that simulates the real world, such as learning about the rainforest by taking a virtual tour in the Amazon rainforest, whereas AR provides learning support to existing content by integrating digital technologies to enhance the educational and learning benefits of the materials. The benefits associated with AR and VR include (a) immersive learning experiences with three-dimensional virtual objects that learners can manipulate to observe and model real-world issues, (b) external visualization of abstract concepts and ideas that are otherwise invisible, (c) implementation of a collaborative learning environment to support real-life problem-solving, and (d) creation of a highly engaging community for sustained learning. The AR/VR experience supports information encoding in working memory and is conducive for retrieving information from long-term memory with a variety of sensory stimuli.

Learning Analytics

Learning analytics (LA), synonymous to educational data mining, is an educational application of web-based technology aimed at learner profiling, a process of gathering and analyzing details of individual student interactions in online learning activities. By gathering data from learners' online activities, the LA predicts the learning path by identifying the learners' knowledge structure and components related to subject domain and indexing the emotional status. The goal is to build better pedagogies, empower active learning, improve the learning performance of struggling students, and assess factors affecting cognitive and affective successes in learning.[183]

There are two types of learning analytics: synchronous and asynchronous. The synchronous analytics obtains students' information during a class. The class can be either online or face-to-face; in the latter case it requires students to be connected through a device. During the class, the teacher might check students' knowledge of the new vocabulary, for example, through LA in a learning management system (LMS) and compare the results with previous performances.

Asynchronous analytics, on the other hand, is the analysis of information outside of class time. The analysis can occur before or after an individual class to predict what students will learn or find out what students have learned. The data collected from learners' online behavior (e.g., when, where, and how many hits in course materials), performance, and communication patterns give insights into the success of the course and enable teachers to make pedagogical decisions about the content, activities, and strategies in instruction.

LA, synchronous or asynchronous, has the ability to gauge learners' performance and offers suggestions for pedagogical adjustment. Based on the outcomes of LA, the teachers are able to adjust the content so that it is challenging but not cognitively overwhelming. In other words, the adjusted contend is, according to Vygotsky, within the learners' zones of proximal development, which optimizes germane cognitive load in learning.[122]

CONCLUSION

The current chapter examines the instructional strategies aimed at optimizing cognitive resources by managing the cognitive load in working memory. The purpose is to identify the roles and cognitive functions of instructional strategies and make connections among types of cognitive load and corresponding instructional strategies.

There are three clusters of instructional strategies identified in this chapter: instructional strategies related to reducing intrinsic cognitive load, lowering extraneous cognitive load, and increasing germane cognitive load. The strategies related to intrinsic cognitive load reduction take the approach of building learners' prior knowledge or schemas to reduce the element interactivity or difficulty level in learning materials. The strategies related to extraneous cognitive load reduction focus on optimizing instruction design to avoid unnecessary processing in learning such as minimizing redundant and split-attention processes. Finally, the strategies related to germane cognitive load center on learner motivation and the design of learning content bordering on the cognitive discomfort zone.

The instructional strategies discussed in this chapter serve as resources that aid teachers in developing cognitively functional instructions to support students' learning. The strategies provide the tools for teachers to reduce learners' intrinsic or extraneous cognitive loads to make cognitive resources available during learning or to increase and maintain germane cognitive loads for effective schemas construction.

FURTHER READING

Chen, O., G. Woolcott, and J. Sweller. "Using Cognitive Load Theory to Structure Computer-Based Learning Including MOOCs." *Journal of Computer Assisted Learning*, 33 (2017): 293–305.

> The article examines massive, open, online course (MOOC) learning from the perspectives of human cognitive architecture and instructional design principles. The paper outlines the theory and indicates instructional design principles that could be used to structure online learning

and to provide an appropriate base for instructional design when using computer-based learning.

Kalyuga, S. *Cognitive Load Factors in Instructional Design for Advanced Learners* (New York: NOVA Science Publishers, 2009).

The book describes the expertise reversal effect in developing instruction from a cognitive load perspective. The author argues that instructional designs and procedures that are cognitively optimal for less knowledgeable learners may not be optimal for more advanced learners. Proposals are made on instructional approaches to optimize cognitive load in learner-tailored, computer-based learning environments.

Kirschner, F., F. Paas, and P. A. Kirschner. "A Cognitive Load Approach to Collaborative Learning: United Brains for Complex Tasks." *Educational Psychology Review* 21, no. 1 (2009): 31–42.

This article compares the effectiveness between individual learning environments and collaborative learning environments. The authors ascribe the differences to differing complexities of the learning tasks and the concomitant load imposed on the learner's cognitive system. The authors describe the cognitive consequences of cognitive load on individual and cooperative learning from a distributed social cognition perspective along with a discussion on the implications of these approaches for research and practices of collaborative learning.

Seufert, T., and R. Brunken. "Cognitive Load and the Format of Instructional Aids for Coherence Formation." *Applied Cognitive Psychology* 20 (2006): 321–331.

The study investigated the process of building referential connections among multiple representations. Several approaches for supporting coherence formation have been examined. An experimental study was carried out to study the strategies about the surface and deep structure referential connections in multiple representations. Results show that coherence formation can be efficiently supported by deep structure support in combination with surface structure support.

Six

Conclusions

Learning, formal or informal, starts with an accumulative process of gathering bits and pieces of information that may appear random at their earliest stages. These seemingly random bits of information originated from our senses become semantically meaningful when they get processed to form mental representations of the external world. The mental representations, often in the form of semantically meaningful concepts like car, food, job, career, and so on get further encoded in long-term memory to become part of our schemas—knowledge structures with which we understand the world. It is obvious that memory plays a key role in the process of learning in our lives. The purpose of this book is to unveil the relationship between memory and learning to inform educators, teachers, and professional trainers of what memory does and how teachers can use memory resources to support students' learning in classrooms.

The book is structured around four major topics: (a) theoretical aspects of memory, (b) memory strategies in education, (c) working memory and related performance factors, and (d) strategies for managing working memory resources, with emphases on understanding the function and role of memories in cognitive information processing.

THEORETICAL ASPECTS OF MEMORY

Memory is a complex construct involving multiple aspects of memory processes. In Chapter Two we start with a framework describing major memory processes pertaining to information encoding and decoding, which include sensory memory, short-term memory, and long-term memory (Figure 2.1). Our discussion shows that sensory memory, which is the shortest-term element of memory, acts as a buffer for external stimuli received from five senses. The information from sensory memory then enters into short-term memory, or working memory, where different sources of information (e.g., audio and visual) are processed and referenced to form mental representations of the new learning material. Some of the information in short-term memory or working memory gets encoded in long-term memory to become part of the knowledge network in the brain. Based on the discussion, we distinguish the coding at each memory by explaining: sensory memory is dominated by sensory codes, working memory is dominated by acoustic and visual codes, and long-term memory is dominated by semantic codes. This distinction is important in that it helps teachers understand the relationship between instructional input and cognitive processes at the memory level. For example, by understanding that sensory information like images and sound supports learners' mental representations, teachers are able to design their instructions for effective sensory and working memory encoding.

In addition, the book includes a description of types of memories that are critical to the functioning of the memories previously discussed, for instance, the relationship between long-term memory and semantic or episodic memory in learning. Because learning can be affected by both our conscious recollection of information (explicit memory) and recall of information previously encoded (implicit memory), a section was devoted to the discussion on explicit and implicit memories and their attributes in learning.

To understand what is exactly involved at the moment of learning, we include a discussion of the cognitive architecture of working memory. A detailed discussion on central executive, phonological loop, and visuo-spatial sketchpad was made with references to their cognitive functions in learning. The discussion provides theoretical support to current practice in multimedia learning where visual, auditory, and haptic modes are used to aid learners' multimode processing of information for deep learning. Further, a discussion of the developmental aspects regarding working memory architecture is included with the purpose of providing educators with the knowledge necessary for developing age-appropriate and cognitively functional instructions.

Finally, the discussion on long-term memory sheds light on the relationship between schema and learning. We learn that long-term memory is a semantic network in which nodes and links represent the semantic information we have acquired through our lives. By taking a developmental perspective, we find that episodic memory, which is memory for personally experienced life events, can evolve into semantic memories. This is interesting because informal learning like visiting a museum, is related to episodic memory, and it can be instructionally optimized to provide the opportunity for building semantic networks. These networks represent the learner's schema, which will be important in later learning.

MEMORY STRATEGIES IN EDUCATION

An important contribution of this book is to link the theoretical discussions on memory to practices in classrooms. Strategies on optimizing the memory functions in information processing are discussed. Chapter Three focuses on four categories of memory strategies: (a) sensory memory, (b) strategies for transferring information from short-term to long-term memory, (c) retrieving information for long-term memory, and (d) metamemory.

Strategies involving sensory memory focus on presenting information with effective use of space, color, and motion. Ambiguous stimuli that lead to misidentification should be avoided. It is recommended that teachers carefully examine the function of sensory stimuli and their support of students' cognitive learning. For example, the use of a red color would effectively capture learners' attention and direct them to important information in the text.

Transferring information from short-term to long-term memory has been the focus of memory strategy research. Chapter Three introduces a slew of memory strategies to support information transitioning from working to long-term memory. The strategies include rehearsal, rereading, distributed and massed practice, categorization, visual imagery, keyword mnemonic, method of loci, and so forth, all of which prove to be effective in transferring information from working to long-term memory. For example, rehearsal has been used to promote knowledge automaticity in skill acquisition like golfing. The strategy of categorization is useful in transferring working memory information to schema construction in long-term memory. The keyword mnemonic is another strategy found to help learners transfer information from working to long-term memory in a variety of subject areas including foreign language vocabulary learning. The many strategies discussed in this book give teachers the option to design their instruction by selecting approaches or techniques that best help students learn. However, teachers should be aware of the issues associated with the strategies as they select the strategy for their teaching. Failing to heed these issues may result in less optimal instruction.

Strategies transferring working memory information to long-term memory represent an encoding process. The encoded information must be retrieved to become useful. In other words, robust learning occurs when knowledge retrieved from long-term memory becomes part of the process in new learning. Strategies related to information retrieval include elaborative interrogation, practice testing, self-explanation, and others. These strategies aim to activate the knowledge in the brain to establish meaningful connections between the knowledge in schema and the learning material. For example, self-explanation requires the learner to engage in self-dialogue to produce adequate explanations of the problems under study. Such a process often involves activation of prior knowledge to make self-explanation intelligent. Teachers may find many retrieval strategies discussed in this book beneficial when they look for ways to activate their students' prior knowledge.

Metamemory is a strategy targeting at learners' metacognitive awareness of their memory abilities, such as what they can remember and what they may forget. The metamemory strategy is important in helping students be strategic about what they learn and how they learn in terms of dealing with the learning demands (e.g., memorization or information retrieval) in classrooms.

WORKING MEMORY AND RELATED PERFORMANCE FACTORS

Working memory is responsible for many of the critical activities in learning. It includes holding information for cognitive processing, generating mental representations, connecting to long-term memory to retrieve information, transferring information to long-term memory to construct schema, and so on. Yet, working memory capacity is limited with a short time duration. Factors such as cognitive overload can easily consume the cognitive resources in working memory and render it less functional.

In Chapter Four we discuss the cognitive factors that influence working memory performance. These factors include intrinsic, extraneous, and germane cognitive load. Intrinsic cognitive load is induced by the content difficulty indicated by high element interactivity. The higher the intrinsic cognitive load, the fewer the cognitive resources in working memory and the worse performance will be in learning. The second factor that affects working memory performance is extraneous cognitive load, which is caused by improper design. In poorly designed instruction, the learner has to spend extra cognitive resources on materials irrelevant to learning. Both intrinsic and extraneous cognitive load are detrimental to learning, and they should be reduced to make cognitive resources available for effective learning. The third type of cognitive load is called germane cognitive load. The germane cognitive load is caused by the mental effort to learn and construct new knowledge. For germane cognitive load to be effective, the extraneous cognitive load must be low, so sufficient cognitive resources are available in working memory for constructing new knowledge.

By identifying the types of cognitive load and their impact on working memory, we show that the performance of working memory can be improved when the deleterious influence caused by intrinsic and extraneous cognitive load is minimized. On that note, developing robust instructional strategies to minimize intrinsic and extraneous cognitive load has significant implications in teaching and learning.

STRATEGIES FOR MANAGING WORKING MEMORY RESOURCES

Given the relationship between cognitive load and working memory performance, a chapter focusing on instructional strategies to manage different types of cognitive load is included. In Chapter Five we include discussions on strategies to reduce intrinsic cognitive load, lower extraneous cognitive load, and increase germane cognitive load for learning.

Our discussion on intrinsic cognitive load reduction focuses on schema construction. It is argued that high prior knowledge lowers element interactivity, thus reducing intrinsic cognitive load. Instructional strategies like pretraining, concept mapping, schema-induced analogical reasoning, worked examples, and cognitive prompts are introduced with empirical evidence showing the effectiveness of these strategies in education. In discussing the strategies for schema construction, several memory strategies mentioned earlier are used to support this effort. For example, the rehearsal strategy is introduced to support learners' knowledge automaticity in an effort to reduce intrinsic cognitive load.

Instructional strategies aiming at lowering extraneous cognitive load are centered on improving the instructional design by eliminating unnecessary cognitive processes in learning such as redundant and split-attention processes. In developing strategies for optimal learning with multimedia, Mayer's theory of multimedia learning is introduced to give guidance on the design of instruction for multimedia learning.

The strategies include visual-visual, visual-audio, and visual-proximity, among others.

A desirable germane cognitive load level is based on the following factors: motivation (for engaged learning), maintenance of an adequate content difficulty (ZPD for constructive learning), and elimination of improper design (to increase cognitive resources). Several strategies are proposed to promote germane cognitive load in learning. They include learner control, self-regulated, multiple perspectives, and collaborative learning to provide the cognitive flexibility and motivation for constructive learning.

Overall, the book provides a systematic overview of the theories and instructional practices in memory. Emphasis is on how the memory research can be used to inform the current practices in education. An in-depth discussion is made with regard to the role of working memory in learning and the instructional strategies enhancing working memory performance by reducing undesirable cognitive load. Teachers and educators will find this book beneficial as it offers both theoretical and practical insights on issues related to memory in education, along with a range of strategies and approaches that will be useful as they implement memory-based strategies in teaching and learning.

Central executive   The central executive controls the flow of information through working memory, retrieves material from long-term memory when necessary, sets goals for the working memory system, and keeps track of what has been accomplished and what needs doing.

Cognitive prompts   Cognitive prompts are an instructional strategy focusing on the activation of and connection with the schema to support meaningful and deep learning. They are learning questions placed throughout an educational presentation that help scaffold learners' thinking processes. Learners become engaged in self-reflection and thinking deeply about the problems with cognitive prompts.

Cognitive resources   Cognitive resources refer to mental resources in the working memory that are used to engage in a variety of cognitive computational thinking in learning, including analysis, application, inferencing, synthesis, and evaluation.

Concept maps   Concept maps are visual representations of a network of ideas and concepts. They reveal patterns and relationships among the concepts and help students clarify their thinking processes while organizing and prioritizing information.

Element interactivity Element interactivity is described as a state in which elements in the learning content interact with each other. High element interactivity indicates a high level of content difficulty.

Episodic memory Episodic memory is memory for personally experienced life events. It is the recollection of past personal experiences that happened at a particular time and place. An example of episodic memory includes remembering a party on a Caribbean cruise years ago.

Explicit memory Explicit memory is the conscious, intentional recollection of factual information, previous experiences, and concepts. Explicit memory is most frequently used in life such as remembering an appointment, recollecting an experience from years ago, and so on.

Extraneous cognitive load Extraneous cognitive load refers to the mental load caused by improper design in instruction. For example, information that is redundant to learning unnecessarily taxes the working memory resources and thus imposes extraneous cognitive load on the learner.

Germane cognitive load Germane cognitive load refers to the mental load induced in learning to construct new knowledge or build a new schema. Unlike extraneous cognitive load, which impedes the learner's learning, germane cognitive load is relevant to learning.

Implicit memory Implicit memory is one of the two main types of long-term memory. It is acquired without consciousness or deliberate recollection and can affect human thoughts and behaviors.

Intrinsic cognitive load Intrinsic cognitive load is induced by the complexity of the content. It refers to the mental load imposed upon the learner's working memory caused by overly complex materials.

Long-term memory Long-term memory differs in significant ways from short-term or working memory. It is extremely large, large enough to contain all of the memories we've accumulated over a lifetime.

Phonological loop The phonological loop appears to be comprised of two separate subcomponents: the phonological store (used to hold phonological information) and the subvocal rehearsal mechanism (used to keep material alive by repeating the sounds in the phonological store). Subvocal rehearsal does not emerge until about seven years of age; prior to that age, only the phonological store is available for verbal memory.

Pretraining Pretraining is an instructional strategy that focuses on schema construction to lower the intrinsic cognitive load in learning.

Rehearsal Rehearsal is a memory strategy in maintaining information in short-term or working memory. It involves repeating information till the information can be retrieved automatically.

Self-regulated learning Self-regulated learning refers to a process of taking control of and evaluating one's own learning behavior, particularly developing learners' metacognitive thinking, strategic action, and motivation to learn.

Semantic memory Semantic memory is our memory of everyday things and how these are organized. It is often referred to as a person's world knowledge that is accumulated over the years. Long-term memory can be thought of as a semantic network in which nodes and links represent the semantic information we have acquired throughout our lives.

Sensory memory Sensory memory stores information received from external sensory stimuli through the five senses: sigh, hearing, smell, taste, and touch. It acts as a kind of buffer for retaining impressions of sensory information after the original external stimulus has ended.

Short-term memory Short-term memory refers to the state of holding a small amount of information in mind in an active short period of time. The duration of short-term memory is believed to be in order of seconds. It can normally holds about 7 ± 2 pieces of information (e.g., letters).

Visual-audio temporal strategy Visual-audio temporal strategy refers to presentation of corresponding information sources (e.g., visual and narration) at the same time in multimedia learning.

Visual proximity strategy

Visual proximity strategy places corresponding words and pictures spatially close to each other. The strategy enables teachers to design and develop effective multimedia, especially visual materials, to support learners' learning.

Visuo-spatial sketchpad

The visuo-spatial sketchpad consists of two components: a visual store that holds the physical characteristics of objects and a spatial mechanism used to plan movements through space and to keep alive the contents of the sketchpad through reactivation (a sort of visual rehearsal).

Worked example

Worked examples mimic the problem steps to support learners' schemata construction in learning. A worked example is a step-by-step demonstration of how to solve the problem.

Working memory

Working memory refers to a memory system that consists of a central executive with two slave systems: phonological loop and visuo-spatial sketchpad. The phonological loop is related to the process of sound, whereas the visual-spatial sketchpad is related to visual-spatial information. The working memory is short with limited capacity. Some people consider short-term memory as different from working memory: The working memory allows for the manipulation of stored information, whereas short-term memory only stores information.

References

1. McCrudden, M.T., & McNamara, D. S. (2018). *Cognition in education*. New York: Routledge.
2. Atkinson, R. C., & Shiffrin, R. M. (1968). Human memory: A proposed system and its control processes. In K. W. Spence & J. T. Spence (Eds.), *The psychology of learning and motivation: Advances in research and theory* (Vol. 2, pp. 89–195). New York: Academic Press.
3. Atkinson, R. C., & Shiffrin, R. M. (1971). The control of short-term memory. *Scientific American*, 225(2), 82–90.
4. Sperling, G. (1960). The information available in brief visual presentations. *Psychological Monographs*, 74(11), 1–29.
5. Averbach, E., & Coriell, A. S. (1961). Short-term memory in vision. *The Bell System Technical Journal*, 40(1), 309–328.
6. Miller, G. A. (1956). The magic number seven, plus or minus two: Some limits on our capacity for processing information. *Psychological Review*, 63(2), 81–97.
7. Brown, J. (1958). Some tests of the decay theory of immediate memory. *Quarterly Journal of Experimental Psychology*, 10(1), 12–21.
8. Peterson, L. R., & Peterson, M. J. (1959). Short-term retention of individual verbal items. *Journal of Experimental Psychology*, 58(3), 193–198.
9. Conrad, R. (1964). Acoustic confusion in immediate memory. *British Journal of Psychology*, 55(1), 75–84.
10. Glass, A. L., & Holyoak, K. J. (1986). *Cognition* (2nd ed.). New York: Random House.
11. Conrad, R. (1972). Short-term memory in the deaf: A test for speech coding. *British Journal of Psychology*, 63(2), 173–180.
12. Craik, F. I. M., & Lockhart, R. S. (1972). Levels of processing: A framework for memory research. *Journal of Verbal Learning and Verbal Behavior*, 11, 671–684.

13. Baddeley, A. D., & Hitch, G. (1974). Working memory. In G. A. Bower (Ed.), *The psychology of learning and motivation* (pp. 47–89). New York: Academic Press.

14. Baddeley, A. D. (1986). *Working memory*. Oxford, UK: Oxford University Press.

15. Baddeley, A. D. (1990). *Human memory: Theory and practice*. Needham Heights, MA: Allyn and Bacon.

16. Brooks, L. R. (1967). The suppression of visualization by reading. *Quarterly Journal of Experimental Psychology, 19*, 289–299.

17. Baddeley, A. D., Grant, S., Wight, E., & Thomson, N. (1975). Imagery and visual working memory. In P. M. A. Rabbitt & S. Dornic (Eds.), *Attention and performance V* (pp. 205–217). London: Academic Press.

18. Baddeley, A. D. (2000). The episodic buffer: A new component of working memory? *Trends in Cognitive Sciences.* 4(11), 417–423.

19. Loftus, E. F., & Loftus, G. R. (1980). On the permanence of stored information in the human brain. *American Psychologist, 35*(5), 409–420.

20. Penfield, W. (1969). Consciousness, memory, and man's conditioned reflexes. In K. H. Pribram (Ed.), *On the biology of learning* (pp. 127–168). New York: Harcourt, Brace, & World.

21. Penfield, W., & Perot, P. (1963). The brain's record of auditory and visual experience: A final discussion and summary. *Brain, 86*, 595–696.

22. Penfield, W., & Roberts, L. (1959). *Speech and brain mechanisms*. Princeton, NJ: Princeton University Press.

23. Crowder, R. G. (1976). *Principles of learning and memory*. Hillsdale, NJ: Lawrence Erlbaum Associates.

24. Brown, R., & McNeill, D. (1966). The 'tip of the tongue' phenomenon. *Journal of Verbal Learning and Verbal Behavior, 5*(4), 325–327.

25. Hart, J. T. (1965). Memory and the feeling of knowing. *Journal of Educational Psychology, 56*(4), 208–216.

26. Tulving, E., & Pearlstone, Z. (1966). Availability versus accessibility of information in memory for words. *Journal of Verbal Learning and Verbal Behavior, 5*(4), 381–391.

27. Anderson, J. R. (1976). *Language, memory, and thought*. Hillsdale, NJ: Lawrence Erlbaum Associates.

28. Anderson, J. R., & Bower, G. H. (1973). *Human associative memory*. New York: John Wiley & Sons.

29. Collins, A. M., & Loftus, E. F. (1975). A spreading activation theory of semantic processing. *Psychological Review*, 82(6), 407–428.

30. Bousfield, W. A. (1953). The occurrence of clustering in the recall of randomly arranged associates. *Journal of General Psychology*, 49, 229–240.

31. Gardner, M. K. (2018). The psychology of deep learning. In R. Z. Zheng (Ed.), *Strategies for deep learning with digital technology: Theories and practice in education* (pp. 3–36). New York: Nova Science Publishers.

32. Fitts, P. M., & Posner, M. I. (1967). *Human performance.* Oxford, UK: Brooks/Cole.

33. Schneider, W., & Shiffrin, R. M. (1977). Controlled and automatic human information processing. I. Detection, search, and attention. *Psychological Review*, 84(1), 1–66.

34. Shiffrin, R. M., & Schneider, W. (1977). Controlled and automatic human information process. II. Perceptual learning, automatic attending, and a general theory. *Psychological Review*, 84(2), 127–190.

35. Kolers, P. A. (1979). A pattern analyzing basis of recognition. In L. S. Cermak & F. I. M. Craik (Eds.), *Levels of processing in human memory* (pp. 363–384). Hillsdale, NJ: Lawrence Erlbaum Associates.

36. Schacter, D. L. (1987). Implicit memory: History and current status. *Journal of Experimental Psychology: Learning, Memory, and Cognition*, 13(3), 501–518.

37. Korsakoff, S. S. (1889). Etude medico-psychologique sur une forme des maladies de la mémoire. *Révue Philosophique*, 28, 501–530.

38. Ebbinghaus, H. (1885). *Über das gedächtnis.* Leipzig: Dunker.

39. Nelson, T. O. (1978). Detecting small amounts of information in memory: Savings for nonrecognized items. *Journal of Experimental Psychology: Human Learning and Memory*, 4(5), 453–468.

40. Roediger, H. L. III. (1990). Implicit memory: Retention without remembering. *American Psychologist*, 45(9), 1043–1056.

41. Warrington, E. K., & Weiskrantz, I. (1968). New method of testing long-term retention with special reference to amnesic patients. *Nature*, 217(5132), 972–974.

42. Warrington, E. K., & Weiskrantz, I. (1970). Amnesic syndrome: Consolidation or retrieval? *Nature*, 228(5272), 629–630.

43. Jacoby, L. L. (1983). Remembering the data: Analyzing interactive processes in reading. *Journal of Verbal Learning and Verbal Behavior*, 22(5) 485–508.

44. Tulving, E. (1972). Episodic and semantic memory. In E. Tulving & W. Donaldson (Eds.), *Organization and memory* (pp. 381–402). Amsterdam: North Holland.

45. Bolla, K. I., Lindgren, K. N., Bonaccorsy, C., & Bleecker, M. L. (1991). Memory complaints in older adults: Fact or fiction? *Archives of Neurology*, 48(1), 61–64.

46. Gardner, M. K., & Hill, R. D. (2013). Training older adults to improve their episodic memory: Three different approaches to enhancing numeric memory. In R. Z. Zheng, R. D. Hill, & M. K. Gardner (Eds.), *Engaging older adults with modern technology: Internet use and information access needs* (pp. 191–211). Hershey, PA: IGI Global.

47. Hulme, C., Muir, C., Thomson, N., & Lawrence, A. (1984). Speech rate and the development of short-term memory span. *Journal of Child Psychology*, 38(2), 241–253.

48. Gathercole, S. E. (1998). The development of memory. *Journal of Child Psychology and Psychiatry*, 39(1), 3–27.

49. Gathercole, S. E., & Hitch, G. J. (1993). Developmental changes in short-term memory: A revised working memory perspective. In A. Collins, S. E. Gathercole, M. A. Conway, & P. E. Morris (Eds.). *Theories of memory* (pp. 189–210). Hove, UK: Psychology Press.

50. Ford, S., & Silber, K. P. (1994). Working memory in children: A developmental approach to the phonological coding of pictorial material. *British Journal of Developmental Psychology*, 12(2), 165–175.

51. Gathercole, S. E., & Adams, A. (1994). Children's phonological working memory: Contributions of long-term knowledge and rehearsal. *Journal of Memory and Language*, 33(5), 672–688.

52. Hitch, G. J., & Halliday, M. S. (1983). Working memory in children. *Philosophical Transactions of the Royal Society, London*, B302, 324–340.

53. Hitch, G. J., Halliday, M. S., Schaafstal, A. M., & Schraagen, J. M. C. (1988). Visual working memory in young children. *Memory and Cognition*, 16(2), 120–132.

54. Longoni, A. M., & Scalisi, T. G. (1994). Developmental aspects of phonemic and visual similarity effects: Further evidence in Italian children. *International Journal of Behavioural Development*, 17(1), 57–71.

55. Hitch, G. J., Halliday, M. S., Dodd, A., & Littler, J. E. (1989). Development of rehearsal in short-term memory: Differences between pictorial and spoken stimuli. *British Journal of Developmental Psychology*, 7(4), 347–362.

56. Wilson, J. L., Scott, J. H., & Powers, K. G. (1987). Developmental differences in the span of visual memory for pattern. *British Journal of Developmental Psychology*, 5(3), 249–255.

57. Kyllonen, P. C., & Christal, R. E. (1990). Reasoning ability is (little more than) working-memory capacity?! *Intelligence*, 14(4), 389–433.

58. Daneman, M., & Carpenter, P. A. (1980). Individual differences in working memory and reading. *Journal of Verbal Learning & Verbal Behavior*, 19(4), 450–466.

59. Case, R., Kurland, D. M., & Goldberg, J. (1982). Operational efficiency and the growth of short-term memory span. *Journal of Experimental Child Psychology*, 33(3), 386–404.

60. Flavell, J. H., Miller, P. H., & Miller, S. A. (1993). *Cognitive development* (3rd ed.). Englewood Cliffs, NJ: Prentice Hall.

61. Kintsch, W. (1970). *Learning, memory, and conceptual processes*. New York: John Wiley & Sons.

62. Chi, M. T. H. (1978). Knowledge structures and memory development. In R. S. Seigler (Ed.), *Children's thinking: What develops?* (pp. 73–150). Hillsdale, NJ: Lawrence Erlbaum Associates.

63. Chase, W. G., & Simon, H. A. (1973). Perception in chess. *Cognitive Psychology*, 4(1), 55–81.

64. Hyde, T. S., & Jenkins, J. J. (1969). Differential effects of incidental tasks on the organization of recall of a list of highly associated words. *Journal of Experimental Psychology*, 83(3), 472–481.

65. Johnston, C. D., & Jenkins, J. J. (1971). Two more incidental tasks that differentially affect associative clustering in recall. *Journal of Experimental Psychology*, 89(1), 92–95.

66. Hartwig, M. K., & Dunlosky, J. (2012). Study strategies of college students: Are self-testing and scheduling related to achievement? *Psychometric Bulletin & Review*, 19(1), 126–134.

67. Dunlosky, J., Rawson, K. A., Marsh, E. J., Nathan, M. J., & Willingham, D. T. (2013). Improving students' learning with effective learning techniques: Promising directions from cognitive and educational psychology. *Psychological Science in the Public Interest*, 14(1), 4–58.

68. Rothkopf, E. Z. (1968). Textual constraint as a function of repeated inspection. *Journal of Educational Psychology*, 59(1, Pt. 1), 20–25.

69. Greeno, J. G. (1964). Paired-associate learning with massed and distributed repetitions of items. *Journal of Experimental Psychology*, 67(3), 286–295.

70. Peterson, L. R., Wampler, R., Kirkpatrick, M., & Saltzman, D. (1963). Effect of spacing presentations on retention of paired-associates over short intervals. *Journal of Experimental Psychology, 66*(2), 206–209.

71. Bahrick, H. P. (1979). Maintenance of knowledge: Questions about memory we forgot to ask. *Journal of Experimental Psychology: General, 108*(3), 296–308.

72. Rawson, K. A., & Kintsch, W. (2005). Rereading effects depend upon the time of test. *Journal of Education, 97*(1), 70–80.

73. Cepeda, N. J., Vul, E., Rohrer, D., Wixted, J. T., & Pashler, H. (2008). Spacing effects in learning: A temporal ridgeline of optimal retention. *Psychological Science, 19*(11), 1095–1102.

74. Justice, E. M. (1985). Categorization as a preferred memory strategy: Developmental changes during elementary school. *Developmental Psychology, 21*(6), 1105–1110.

75. Bousfield, W. A., Cohen, B. H., & Whitmarsh, G. A. (1958). Associative clustering in the recall of words of different taxonomic frequencies of occurrence. *Psychological Report, 4*, 39–44.

76. Cohen, B. H. (1966). Some-or-none characteristics of coding behavior. *Journal of Verbal Learning and Verbal Behavior, 5*(2), 182–187.

77. Cofer, C. N. (1965). On some factors in the organizational characteristics of free recall. *American Psychologist, 20*(4), 261–272.

78. Shepard, R. N. (1967). Recognition memory for words, sentences, and pictures. *Journal of Verbal Learning and Verbal Behavior, 6*(1), 156–163.

79. Bower, G. H. (1972). Mental imagery and associative learning. In L. W. Gregg (Ed.), *Cognition in learning and memory* (pp. 51–88). New York: John Wiley & Sons.

80. Raugh, M. R., & Atkinson, R. C. (1975). A mnemonic method for learning a second-language vocabulary. *Journal of Educational Psychology, 67*(1), 1–16.

81. Wang, A. Y., Thomas, M. H., & Ouellette, J. A. (1992). Keyword mnemonic and retention of second-language vocabulary words. *Journal of Educational Psychology, 84*(4), 520–528.

82. Bower, G. H. (1970). Analysis of a mnemonic device: Modern psychology uncovers the powerful components of an ancient system for improving memory. *American Scientist, 58*(5), 496–510.

83. Leutner, D., Leopold, C., & Sumfleth, E. (1975). Cognitive load and science text comprehension: Effects of drawing and mentally imaging text content. *Computers in Human Behavior, 25*(2), 284–289.

84. de Beni, R., & Moè, A. (2003). Presentation modality effects in studying passages. Are mental images always effective? *Applied Cognitive Psychology, 17*(3), 309–324.

85. Levin, J. R., & Divine-Hawkins, P. (1974). Visual imagery as a prose-learning process. *Journal of Reading Behavior, 6*(1), 23–30.

86. Denis, M. (1982). Imaging while reading text: A study of individual differences. *Memory & Cognition, 10*(6), 540–545.

87. Cioffi, G. (1986). Relationships among comprehension strategies reported by college students. *Reading Research and Instruction, 25*(3), 220–231.

88. Gurung, R. A. R., Weidert, J., & Jeske, A. (2010). Focusing on how students study. *Journal of the Scholarship of Teaching and Learning, 10*(1), 28–35.

89. Fowler, R. L., & Barker, A. S. (1974). Effectiveness of highlighting for retention of text material. *Journal of Applied Psychology, 59*(3), 358–364.

90. Bretzing, B. H., & Kulhavy, R. W. (1979). Notetaking and depth of processing. *Contemporary Educational Psychology, 4*(2), 145–163.

91. Tulving, E., & Osler, S. (1968). Effectiveness of retrieval cues in memory for words. *Journal of Experimental Psychology, 77*(4), 593–601.

92. Tulving, E., & Thomson, D. M. (1973). Encoding specificity and retrieval processes in episodic memory. *Psychological Review, 80*(5), 352–373.

93. Gordon, F. R., & Flavell, J. H. (1977). The development of intuitions about cognitive cueing. *Child Development, 48*(3), 1027–1033.

94. Bower, G. H. (1981). Mood and memory. *American Psychologist, 36*(2), 129–148.

95. Bower, G. H., Gilligan, S. G., & Monteiro, K. P. (1981). Selective learning caused by affective state. *Journal of Experimental Psychology: General, 110*(4), 451–473.

96. Bower, G. H., Monteiro, K. P., & Gilligan, S. G. (1978). Emotional mood as a context for learning and recall. *Journal of Verbal Learning and Verbal Behavior, 17*(5), 573–585.

97. Pressley, M., McDaniel, M. A., Turnure, J. E., Wood, E., & Ahmad, M. (1987). Generation and precision of elaboration: Effects on intentional and incidental learning. *Journal of Experimental Psychology: Learning, Memory, and Cognition, 13*(2), 291–300.

98. Minsky, M. (June, 1974). *A framework for representing knowledge.* Cambridge, MA: MIT-AI Laboratory Memo 306.

99. Schank, R. C., & Abelson, R. P. (1977). *Scripts, plans, goals, and understanding.* Hillsdale, NJ: Lawrence Erlbaum Associates.

100. Bartlett, F. C. (1932). *Remembering*. Cambridge, UK: Cambridge University Press.

101. Rawson, K. A., & Dunlosky, J. (2011). Optimizing schedules of retrieval practice for durable and efficient learning: How much is enough? *Journal of Experimental Psychology: General*, 140(3), 283–302.

102. Roediger, H. L. III, & Butler, A. C. (2011). The critical role of retrieval practice in long-term retention. *Child Development*, 77(1), 1–15.

103. Roediger, H. L. III, Putnam, A. L., & Smith, M. A. (2011). Ten benefits . B. H. Ross (Eds.), *The psychology of learning and motivation* (Vol. 55, pp. 1–36). San Diego, CA: Elsevier Academic Press.

104. Pyc, M. A., & Rawson, K. A. (2010). Why testing improves memory: Mediator effectiveness hypothesis. *Science*, 330(6002), 335.

105. Pyc, M. A., & Rawson, K. A. (2012). Why is test-restudy practice beneficial for memory? An evaluation of the mediator shift hypothesis. *Journal of Experimental Psychology: Learning, Memory, and Cognition*, 38(3), 737–746.

106. Hunt, R. R. (1995). The subtlety of distinctiveness: What von Restorff really did. *Psychonomic Bulletin & Review*, 2(1), 105–112.

107. Hunt, R. R. (2006). The concept of distinctiveness in memory research. In R. R. Hunt & J. B. Worthen (Eds.), *Distinctiveness and memory* (pp. 3–25). New York: Oxford University Press.

108. Ainsworth, S., & Burcham, S. (2007). The impact of text coherence on learning by self-explanation. *Learning and Instruction*, 17(3), 286–303.

109. Wong, R. M. F., Lawson, M. J., & Keeves, J. (2002). The effects of self-explanation training on students' problem solving in high-school mathematics. *Learning and Instruction*, 12(2), 233–262.

110. Beal, C. R. (1985). Development of knowledge about the use of cues to aid prospective retrieval. *Child Development*, 56(3), 631–642.

111. Flavell, J. H., Friedrichs, A. G., & Hoyt, J. D. (1970). Developmental changes in memorization processes. *Cognitive Psychology*, 1(4), 324–340.

112. Worden, P. E., & Sladewski-Awig, L. J. (1982). Children's awareness of memorability. *Journal of Educational Psychology*, 74(3), 341–350.

113. Wellman, H. M. (1977). Preschoolers' understanding of memory-relevant variables. *Developmental Psychology*, 48(4), 1720–1723.

114. Tenney, Y. J. (1975). The child's conception of organization and recall. *Journal of Experimental Child Development*, 19(1), 100–114.

115. Kreutzer, M. A., Leonard, C., & Flavell, J. H. (1975). An interview study of children's knowledge about memory. *Monographs of the Society for Research in Child Development, 40* (1, Serial No. 159).

116. Van Merrienboer, J. J. G., & Sweller, J. (2005). Cognitive load theory and complex learning: Recent developments and future directions. *Educational Psychology Review, 17*(2), 147–177.

117. Sweller, J., & Chandler, P. (1991). Evidence for cognitive load theory. *Cognition and Instruction, 8*(4), 351–362.

118. Sweller, J., & Chandler, P. (1994). Why some material is difficult to learn. *Cognition and Instruction, 12*(3), 185–233.

119. Sweller, J., van Merrienboer, J. J., & Paas, F. G. (1998). Cognitive architecture and instructional design. *Educational Psychological Review, 10,* 251–296.

120. Mayer, R. E. (2001). *Multimedia learning.* Cambridge, UK: Cambridge University Press.

121. Mayer, R. E., & Moreno, R. (2003). Nine ways to reduce cognitive load in multimedia learning. *Educational Psychologist, 38*(1), 43–52.

122. Sweller, J. (2018). The role of independent measures of load in cognitive load theory. In R. Zheng (ed.), *Cognitive load measurement and application: A theoretical framework for meaningful research and practice* (pp. 1–8). New York: Routledge.

123. Vygotsky, L. S. (1978). *Mind in society: The development of higher psychological processes.* Cambridge, MA: Harvard University Press.

124. Schnotz, W. (2010). Reanalyzing the expertise reversal effect. *Instructional Science, 38,* 315–323.

125. Um, E. R., Plass, J. L., Hayward, E. O., & Homer, B. D. (2012). Emotional design in multimedia learning. *Journal of Educational Psychology, 104*(2), 485–498.

126. Dinsmore, D. L. (2018). *Strategic processing in education.* New York: Routledge.

127. Paivio, A. (1986). *Mental representations: A dual coding approach.* Oxford, UK: Oxford University Press.

128. Pollock, E., Chandler, P., & Sweller, J. (2002). Assimilating complex information. *Learning and Instruction, 12,* 61–86.

129. Zheng, R., Gupta, U., & Dewald, A. (2012). Does the format of pretraining matter? A study on the effects of different pretraining approaches on prior knowledge construction in an online

environment. *International Journal of Cyber Behavior, Psychology and Learning*, 2(2), 35–47.

130. Kinchin, I. M., & Hay, D. B. (2000). How a qualitative approach to concept map analysis can be used to aid learning by illustrating patterns of conceptual development? *Educational Research*, 42(1), 43–57.

131. Puntambekar, S., & Goldstein, J. (2007). Effect of visual representation of the conceptual structure for learning from computer-based science simulations. *Journal of Educational Multimedia and Hypermedia*, 16(4), 429–459.

132. Roberts, V., & Joiner, R. (2007). Investigating the efficacy of concept mapping with pupils with autistic spectrum disorder. *British Journal of Special Education*, 34(3), 127–135.

133. Nesbit, J. C., & Adesope, O. O. (2006). Learning with concept and knowledge maps: A meta-analysis. *Review of Educational Research*, 76(3), 413–448.

134. Sweller, J., & Cooper, G. A. (1985). The use of worked example as a substitute for problem solving in learning algebra. *Cognition and Instruction*, 12(1), 59–89.

135. Booth, J. L., Lange, K. E., Koedinger, K. R., & Newton, K. J. (2013). Using example problems to improve student learning in algebra: Differentiating between correct and incorrect examples. *Learning and Instruction*, 25, 24–34.

136. Van Gog, T., Paas, F., & Van Merrienboer, J. J. G. (2006). Effects of process oriented worked example on trouble shooting transfer performance. *Learning and Instruction*, 16, 154–164.

137. Richey, J. E., & Nokes-Malch, T. J. (2013). How much is too much? learning and motivation effects of adding instructional explanations to worked example. *Learning and Instruction*, 25, 104–124.

138. Kaluga, S. (2007). Expertise reversal effect and its implications for learner-tailored instruction. *Educational Psychology Review*, 19, 509–539.

139. Kalyuga, S., Chandler, P., & Sweller, J. (1998). Levels of expertise and instructional design. *Human Factors: The Journal of the Human Factors and Ergonomics Society*, 40(1), 1–17.

140. Gentner, D., & Gentner, D. R. (1983). Flowing waters or teeming crowds: Mental models of electricity. In D. Gentner & A. L. Stevens (Eds.), *Mental models* (pp. 99–129). Hillsdale, NJ: Lawrence Erlbaum.

141. Sternberg, R. J. (1977). Component processes in analogical reasoning. *Psychological Review*, 84, 353–378.

142. Holyoak, K. J., & Thagard, P. (1989). Analogical mapping by constraint satisfaction. *Cognitive Science, 13,* 295–355.

143. Zheng, R., Yang, W., Garcia, D., & McCadden, B. P. (2008). Effects of multimedia on schema induced analogical reasoning in science learning. *Journal of Computer Assisted Learning, 24,* 474–482.

144. Berthold, K., Nuckles, M., & Renkl, A. (2007). Do learning protocols support learning strategies and outcomes? The role of cognitive and metacognitive prompts. *Learning and Instruction, 17,* 564–577.

145. Smith, D., Zheng, R., Metz, A. J., Morrow, S., Pompa, J., Hill, J., & Rupper, R. (2019). Role of cognitive prompts in video caregiving training for older adults: Optimizing deep and surface learning. *Educational Gerontology, 45*(1), 45–56.

146. Zheng, R. (2018). Understanding the functional roles of multimodal processing and Gc activation in older people's performance in caregiving training. *OBM Geriatrics, 2*(4), 26.

147. Goldstein, B. E. (2008). Cognitive psychology: Connecting mind, research, and everyday experience (2nd ed.). Belmont, CA: Thomas Wadsworth.

148. van Merriënboer, J. J. G. (1997). *Training complex cognitive skills: A four-component instructional design model for technical training.* Englewood Cliffs, NJ: Educational Technology Publications.

149. Clark, R. C., Nguyen, F., & Sweller, J. (2006). *Efficiency in learning: Evidence-based guidelines to manage cognitive load.* San Francisco, CA: Pfeiffer.

150. Ioannou, P., Rodiou, E., & Iliou, T. (2017). Pictures with narration versus pictures with on-screen text during teaching mathematics. *Research in Pedagogy, 7*(1), 57–68.

151. Tindall-Ford, S., Chandler, P., & Sweller, J. (1997). When two sensory modes are better than one. *Journal of Experimental Psychology: Applied, 3*(4), 257–287.

152. Mayer, R. E., & Johnson, C. I. (2008). Revising the redundancy principle in multimedia learning. *Journal of Educational Psychology, 100*(2), 380–386.

153. Mayer, R. E., Steinhoff, B. G., & Mars, R. (1995). A generative theory of textbook design: Using annotated illustrations to foster meaningful learning of science text. *Educational Technology Research & Development, 43,* 31–43.

154. Moreno, R., & Mayer, R. E. (1999). Cognitive principles of multimedia learning: The role of modality and contiguity. *Journal of Educational Psychology*, 91, 358–368.

155. Mayer, R. E., & Anderson, R. B. (1992). The instructive animation: Helping students build connections between words and pictures in multimedia learning. *Journal of Educational Psychology*, 84, 444–452.

156. Mayer, R. E., Moreno, R., Boire, M., & Vagge, S. (1999). Maximizing constructivist learning from multimedia communications by minimizing cognitive load. *Journal of Educational Psychology*, 91, 638–643.

157. de Koning, B. B., Tabbers, H. K., Rikers, R. M. J. P., & Paas, F. (2007). Attention cueing as a means to enhance learning from an animation. *Applied Cognitive Psychology*, 21, 731–746.

158. Tabbers, H. K., Martens, R. L., & van Merrienboer, J. J. G. (2004). Multimedia instructions and cognitive load theory: Effects of modality and cueing. *British Journal of Educational Psychology*, 74, 71–81.

159. Richter, J., Scheiter, K., & Eitel, A. (2018). Signaling text-picture relations in multimedia learning: The influence of prior knowledge. *Journal of Educational Psychology*, 110, 544–560.

160. Sweller, J. (2005). Implications of cognitive load theory for multimedia learning. In R. E. Mayer (Ed.), *The Cambridge handbook of multimedia learning* (pp. 19–30). New York: Cambridge University Press.

161. Liu, M., Toprac, P., & Yuen, T. T. (2009). What factors make a multimedia learning environment engaging: A case study. In R. Zheng (Ed.), *Cognitive effects of multimedia learning* (pp. 173–192). Hershey, PA: Information Science Reference/IGI Global.

162. Gupta, U. (2018). Managing cognitive during complex learning: A study on worked examples and element interactivity. *Dissertation Abstracts International*, 78(10-A)E.

163. Sunawan, & Xiong, J. (2017). The impact of control belief and learning disorientation on cognitive load: The mediating effect of academic emotions in two types of hypermedia learning environments. *Turkish Online Journal of Educational Technology*, 16(1), 177–189.

164. Chang, C., Liang, C., Chou, P., & Lin, G. (2017). Is game-based learning better in flow experience and various types of cognitive load than non-game-based learning? Perspective from multimedia and media richness. *Computers in Human Behavior*, 71, 218–227.

165. Zimmerman, B. J., & Schunk, D. H. (2011). *Handbook of self-regulation of learning and performance.* New York: Taylor & Francis.

166. Bankbaar, M. E. W., Alsma, J., Jansen, E. E. H., van Merrienboer, J. J. G., van Saase, J. L., C. M., & Schuit, S. C. E. (2016). An experimental study on the effects of a simulation game on students' clinical cognitive skills and motivation. *Advances in Health Science Education*, 21, 505–521.

167. Cleary, T. J., & Kitsantas, A. (2017). Motivation and self-regulated learning influences on middle school mathematics achievement. *School Psychology Review*, 46, 88–107.

168. MacArthur, C. A., Philippakos, Z. A., & Ianetta, M. (2015). Self-regulated strategy instruction in college developmental writing. *Journal of Educational Psychology*, 107, 855–867.

169. Cook, D. A., Castillo, R. M., Gas, B., & Artino, A. R. (2017). Measuring achievement goal motivation, mindsets and cognitive load: Validation of three instruments' scores. *Medical Education*, 51, 1061–1074.

170. Kalyuga, S. (2009). Instructional designs for the development of transferable knowledge and skills: A cognitive load perspective. *Computers in Human Behavior*, 25, 332–338.

171. Baars, M., Wijnia, L., & Paas, F. (2017). The association between motivation, affect, and self-regulated learning when solving problems. *Frontier in Psychology*, 8, Article 1346.

172. Peters, S., Clarebout, G., van Nuland, M., Aertgeerts, B., & Roex, A. (2018). A qualitative exploration of multiple perspectives on transfer of learning between classroom and clinical workplace. *Teaching and Learning in Medicine*, 30(1), 22–32.

173. Hutchins, E. (1995). *Cognition in the wild.* Cambridge, MA: MIT Press.

174. Vasciliou, C., Loannou, A., Stylianou-Georgiou, A., & Zaphiris, P. (2017). A glance into social and evolutionary aspects of an artifact ecology for collaborative learning through the lens of distributed cognition. *International Journal of Human-Computer Interaction*, 33(8), 642–654.

175. Chen, C. H., Wang, K. C., & Lin, Y. H. (2015). The comparison of solitary and collaborative modes of game-based learning on students' science learning and motivation. *Journal of Educational Technology & Society*, 18(2), 237–248.

176. Retnowati, E., Ayres, P., & Sweller, J. (2017). Can collaborative learning improve the effectiveness of worked examples in learning mathematics? *Journal of Educational Psychology*, 109(5), 666–679.

177. Soller, A. (2001). Supporting social interaction in an intelligent collaborative learning system. *International Journal of Artificial Intelligence in Education, 12,* 40–62.

178. Wang, M., & Hwang, G. (2017). A problem posing-based practicing strategy for facilitating students' computer programming skills in the team-based learning mode. *Educational Technology Research & Development, 65,* 1655–1671.

179. Butcher, K., Rumberg, M., & Altizer, R. (2017). Dino lab: Designing and developing an educational game for critical thinking. In R. Zheng & M. Gardner (Eds.), *Handbook of research on serious games for educational applications* (pp. 115–148). Hershey, PA: IGI Global.

180. Thompson, N., Peppler, K., & Danish, J. (2017). Designing BioSim: Playfully encouraging systems thinking in young children. In R. Zheng & M. Gardner (Eds.), *Handbook of research on serious games for educational applications* (pp. 149–167). Hershey, PA: IGI Global.

181. Lee, J., & Liu, M. (2017). Design of fantasy and their effects on learning and engagement in a serious game. In R. Zheng & M. Gardner (Eds.), *Handbook of research on serious games for educational applications* (pp. 197–216). Hershey, PA: IGI Global.

182. Poitras, E., Harley, J. M., Compeau, T., Kee, K., & Lajoie, S. P. (2017). Augmented reality to informal learning settings: Leveraging technology for the love of history. In R. Zheng & M. Gardner (Eds.), *Handbook of research on serious games for educational applications* (pp. 272–293). Hershey, PA: IGI Global.

183. Zheng, R., & Greenberg, K. (2018). Effective design in human and machine learning: A cognitive perspective. In F. Chen & J. Zhou (eds.), *Human and machine learning:Visible, explainable, trustworthy and transparent* (pp. 55–74). New York: Springer.

Index